BRIAN CLOUGH
AND
DERBY COUNTY
From Glory to Disaster

BRIAN CLOUGH
AND
DERBY COUNTY

From Glory to Disaster

*The inside story as told by
the DCFC Board Meeting Minutes*

ANDY ELLIS

First Published in Great Britain in 2017 by DB Publishing,
an imprint of JMD Media Ltd

ISBN 978-1-78091-548-7

Printed and bound in the UK

CONTENTS

INTRODUCTION

It is now 45 years since Derby County Football Club became the Champions of England for the first time, under the guidance of the managerial partnership of Brian Clough and Peter Taylor, presided over by Chairman Sam Longson. As champions, they took their place in the European Cup for the first time and progressed through to the semi-final before being knocked out in controversial circumstances by Juventus of Italy. Within six months of that game, the managerial partnership's long-running disagreements with Chairman Sam Longson and the majority of the Board of Directors saw the duo resign (not for the first time). They were shortly afterwards replaced by former player, and then current Nottingham Forest Manager, Dave Mackay.

Sam Longson maintained that the three most important men in any football club are (in alphabetical order) the Chairman, Manager and Secretary. All three positions carry their own responsibilities and roles that must be fulfilled to ensure the smooth running of any club, and they all must come together and work collectively for the benefit of the Club. As soon as that circle of trust and communication is broken, problems will arise.

The number of football-related books (whether biographies, autobiographies, 'complete records', Who's Who or photographic records) has increased vastly since the 1980s, and many former Rams players – including Dave Mackay, Roy McFarland, Colin Todd, John McGovern and Archie Gemmill, management duo Brian Clough and Peter Taylor, Secretary Stuart Webb and Chairman Sam Longson – have all written their autobiographies with their own view and perspective of those events of the early 1970s. The one viewpoint missing from that list is that of the football club itself.

This book contains the details of all the major events that happened in and around the football club from the start of the 1970–71 season through to the autumn of 1973, as recorded in the official pages of the minute books, together with my additional notes that cover other off-the-field events and other issues surrounding the Club that will explain some of the actions and comments made in those Minutes.

Derby County's Board Meetings generally took place every week, usually on a Thursday at the Baseball Ground. The format of the meetings usually followed a set pattern, which comprised of the Manager (or Assistant Manager) being called in for a portion of it to report on playing matters, player issues and transfers, and then other Club matters such as the stadium, finance and any other matters arising for the remaining time. Not every page or minute has been reproduced for every meeting, or complete meetings, as some relate to share transfers where names and addresses are used and also some do not have anything of interest to share with the reader. The Minutes are, as with any set of Minutes for any organisation, a condensed summary of the discussion that took place and any actions arising. They do not record the detail of those talks or arguments.

The objective here is to provide some background to the events of those three years and, while not in any way wishing to diminish the on-field achievements of the players and management at this time, to show that behind the scenes the Board of Directors and administration of the club had a difficult task maintaining control, and no matter what they did, or could do, they would be seen as villains in the eyes of the public.

The years covered in this book look at the last three of most successful period in the club's history with the Second Division title, First Division title, Central League, Watney Cup, Texaco Cup all won and appearances in the League Cup and European Cup semi-finals all within the six years of the tenure of Brian Clough and Peter Taylor.

In order to create this, I have been granted exclusive and unique access to the Board Meeting Minutes, courtesy of the football club. I hope that it adds to the documented history of the Club of that period, and that the reader can form their own opinion of what was happening behind the scenes and the actions taken by all parties concerned.

We start in controversial circumstances, with the club receiving a European ban for administrative failings, and go through the three complete seasons step by step as record-breaking transfers take place, illegal approaches are made to players, and cheating referees potentially deny them a place at the European Cup Final in 1973.

As we move into September and October of 1973, we begin to look more closely at the many events surrounding the Club at that time, and the various meetings taking place behind the scenes in the lead-up to the departure of the management duo. This then sparked talk of player revolts, protest marches through the streets, and the subsequent movement to try and reverse the decision to accept their resignations.

One can only speculate what may have happened if the decision had been reversed – would the following years have been as successful? How long before the next major argument with the Board, or the next resignation or tempting job offer came along? Would the transfer record be broken again, as players were replaced? Maybe for another book, another time.

Up the Rams!

Andy Ellis

Summer 2017

ACKNOWLEDGEMENTS

This book would not have been possible but for the work behind the scenes of a number of people and organisations that I am grateful to, for their time and efforts in getting this published. First and foremost are the Directors of Derby County Football Club, who have allowed these Minutes to be viewed and read by the general football fan for the first time. Who knows – depending upon the success or otherwise of this book, the door maybe be open to repeat the format for other years.

I have dealt with Steve and Jane Caron at JMD Media (and previously at Breedon Books) since 2005 with my first publication *Relics of the Rams*, and Steve has been in regular touch regarding this book ever since I showed him scans of the original Minutes, and without their backing it would not have been possible. Dan Coxon has put the final version together in the format you are holding.

Once again thanks to my father, John, who took me to see my first game way back in 1969, in guidance and making sure I stick to the facts and do not drift off into random stories or unproven details. I should also say thank you to Peter Bonnell, Senior Curator at Quad in Derby and Trustee of The Derby County Collection, who performed a similar first-pass sense check of the text. Andy Dawson also provided the missing scores from various pre-season friendly matches that are listed – these being particularly difficult to track down.

Other background information included in the book has come from the Club's own newspaper/programme, *The Ram*, that was issued for each match during this time, and also the online newspaper library of the *Daily Express* and *Daily Mirror*, which were used for the confirmation of dates.

All the photographic images used in the book originated from Raymonds Press Agency which went into liquidation in October 2010. Their back catalogue of prints and negatives was sold (with copyright) at auction, which is where these were obtained from.

Finally, none of this would be worth reading and there would be no story to tell without the best football management duo that have worked in British football and the wonderful set of players they assembled that took on and beat the best teams in England (including many of the world's best players at that time), and also made a name for themselves all over Europe and wider afield. Even today, 45 years after the events written here, those players are held in high esteem by Derby County fans, with Roy McFarland now a Director of the club and Roger Davies one of the Club's ambassadors.

WHO'S WHO

The Board of Directors

Sam Longson, Chairman

Based in Chapel-en-le-Frith in north Derbyshire, Longson owned a successful, specialist haulage company. He became a Director of the Club in 1953 and was elected Chairman in 1967, and brought in the management duo of Brian Clough and Peter Taylor from Hartlepool United.

He took over the chairmanship again in 1970 after the League/FA investigation into the administration of the Club and continued until February 1977, by which time he had guided the Club to two League Championship titles, a European Cup semi-final, League Cup semi-final and FA Cup semi-final. He was awarded the OBE in the 1977 New Year's Honours List.

He was well known for his trilby hat, his love of cigars, and, unusually, he had a large collection of teapots that he was able to add to whilst travelling with the team across Europe.

Sir (Clifford) Robertson King, KBE

Sir Robertson King had been a Director of the football club since 1950, and was Chairman in the late 1950s and was elected President in 1961.

He had been the General Manager of the Derby and Notts Electricity Power Company since 1938, until it was nationalised, when he then became Chairman of the East Midlands Electricity Board as part of the nationalisation programme. In 1959, he was promoted to the top job in the industry – Chairman of the Electricity Council, where he remained until his retirement.

The New Year's Honours List of 1954 saw him awarded the CBE, and he became a KBE in June 1960.

Mr Fred B. Walters

Mr F. B. Walters had been a Director for 22 years and was Vice-President until his death in 1972, and was a daily visitor to the ground.

He had been the Chairman and Managing Director of a local roofing company, John Shenton Limited, and had joined the Board in 1950. He held the post of Chairman of the football club for four years from December 1959, taking over from Sir Robertson King.

Mr Bill Rudd

Rudd was one of the newest Directors to be appointed, joining in May 1970, and was a member of the Finance and Promotion Committees and had been a supporter for more than 50 years.

Professionally, he was a legal executive with a firm of solicitors and his legal knowledge and background was of a big benefit to the Club, as more and more complex matters arose as the Club reached new heights at home and abroad.

Mr Sydney C. Bradley

He owned a menswear clothing shop on East Street, Derby selling ready-made suits and accessories. He joined the Board in December 1960. He was Chairman at the time when the Club was promoted from the Second Division in 1969, and was Vice-Chairman throughout the early 1970s. He became a Vice-President along with Sam Longson on the death of Fred Walters in 1972.

He was also a member of the Finance Committee.

Mr Bob Innes

He left the British Army just in time to be able to see the 1946 FA Cup Final victory against Charlton Athletic, and joined the Board in May 1970.

He was a senior partner in his family-run business, Innes and Sons, who were chartered surveyors and estate agents.

He was a member of the Promotions Committee as the Club sought new means of funding outside of the matchday gate receipts.

Mr Michael Keeling

He was the youngest member of the Board, joining in May 1970 along with Bill Rudd and Frank Innes, and had similar responsibilities in the Promotions Committee to raise funds.

He resigned from the Board at the same time as Clough and Taylor, and was a driving force in the *Bring Back Clough* protest movement.

Mr Jack Kirkland

He was the brother of Robert Kirkland, who was on the Board until the summer of 1970 when he was forced out by Sam Longson.

He was Chairman of the family-owned, Heage-based construction and engineering firm, Bowmer & Kirkland. His son, John, became a Director of the Club from 1981–2002 and was re-appointed in June 2017. Jack Kirkland came onto the Board in 1973 and his industry-leading knowledge of building safety meant that the Club had access to someone who could ensure that the stadium, so long neglected, was one of the safest in the country. At the time of his appointment he was the largest shareholder in the Club.

Administration – Club Secretary

Mr Stuart Webb

He was Assistant Secretary at Preston North End and was making a name for himself and attracting the attention of several First Division clubs. He was brought down to Derby and given the Secretary's position by Brian Clough, without the knowledge of the Chairman who was away on holiday at the time. Stuart was to have a long and distinguished career at Derby, being Chief Executive for many years, and was the main driving force that kept the Club from going into liquidation in 1984, brokering a deal with Robert Maxwell to save the Club. He remained heavily involved with the Club until he sold his business, Lonsdale Travel, in 2003 and relocated to Spain.

Football Management

Mr Brian Clough

Clough was a prolific goal scorer for Sunderland and Middlesbrough until a severe knee injury prematurely finished his playing career at the age of 29. Once recovered, he became part of the Sunderland Youth coaching team and coached John O'Hare and Colin Todd. He took the Manager's job at Hartlepool United in 1965, the youngest Manager in the Football League. Having established himself, two years later he was approached to be the new Manager of Derby County when Tim Ward's contract was not renewed. After resigning at Derby, he went to Brighton (32 games) and then the famous 44 days at Leeds United, before finishing up at Nottingham Forest where he stayed for nearly 18 years and nearly 1000 matches.

Mr Peter Taylor

Taylor was a goalkeeper for Middlesbrough and in the same team as Clough. He was invited to join Clough at Hartlepool and left his post as Manager of Burton Albion. The pair formed a unique partnership and we were to stay together, although there were often stories of rifts and arguments, until 1982 when he re-joined Derby as Manager and the pair fell out totally over Derby's signing of John Robertson from Forest. He followed Clough to Brighton, but refused to go to Leeds with him and continued until July 1976 when the partnership was reformed at Forest.

SEASON 1970–71

The 1969–70 season had been Derby's first in the top division since the early 1950s, and with the same team that won the Second Division title comfortably the year before, they embarked upon their latest adventure, this time playing at Old Trafford, Highbury, Anfield and White Hart Lane instead of Brunton Park (Carlisle), Manor Ground (Oxford) and Gigg Lane (Bury).

During that fabulous first season the Club saw the opening of the new Ley Stand, built above the Popular Side terracing, the first major change to the stadium for nearly 40 years, and on the field performances saw them go unbeaten for the first 13 games. During the season, there were famous victories against well-established teams full of the England World Cup winning team of 1966, and those battling to be on the flight to Mexico for the Finals in the summer of 1970.

Those famous wins included a 5–0 drubbing of Tottenham Hotspur, 2–0 against Manchester United and 4–0 v. Liverpool, also setting a Club record attendance figure of 41,826 against Tottenham Hotspur and five other attendances of over 40,000 against Manchester United, Manchester City, Liverpool, Sheffield United and Leeds United during that first season.

The effect that Clough had on the fortunes of the Club had already brought in offers for his services from other clubs, notably Barcelona in November 1969 and the Greek National team in May 1970, neither of which amounted to anything more than passing interest.

The rapid rise from a mid-lower Second Division club to one finishing fourth in the First Division within a couple of years under Brian Clough brought with it an increase in money flowing into the Club, and a much bigger media profile, and they became victims of their own success with the small and inexperienced administration department of the Club failing to keep up with the demand and success. Clough had appointed the 21-year-old Assistant Secretary from Sunderland, Malcolm Bramley, as Club Secretary, and without proper administrative support the job was not suitable for someone of his level of experience.

Problems surfaced in the accounts, which showed that £55,000 had gone missing and could not be accounted for, and the footballing authorities started investigations into the wider procedures at the Club.

The investigating joint committee from the Football Association and Football League decided that there were eight charges that could be brought against the Club:

1. Rule 44 (a) had been contravened with regard to discrepancies in Club finance.

2. Rule 25 (a) – registration of players; 26 (b) – payment to agents; 27 (a) – permit players had been contravened.

3. Breach of rule 27 (a) and 40 (a) – variation of payments during the season without approval.

4. Breach of rule 27 (a) and 42 – Frank Wignall, John Richardson and Les Green's contracts had not been lodged with the authorities.

5. Breach of rule 42 – payment to Dave Mackay for writing programme notes was against the Management Committee ruling.

6. Breach of rule 25(a) – junior players taking part in trial games were amateur players.

7. Breach of rule 47 – lodging allowances for apprentices.

8. Breach of rule 27 (a) and 47 – amount was missing from Mackay's contract.

'The commission reached the conclusion that there had been gross negligence in the administration of the Club … took cognisance of the fact that steps had been taken to correct this maladministration prior to the investigation into the affairs of the Club being undertaken.'

Manchester United were found guilty a year previously and fined £7,000 and banned from European competitions for a year. The extent of Derby's misaccounting was so serious that relegation was one possible punishment that could have been considered (and had been used before, against Port Vale and Peterborough United, for lesser offences) before settling on a record-breaking £10,000 fine and a ban on playing in European competitions or playing any friendly against a club outside the control of the Football Association until 30 April 1971. Having finished fourth in the table, this meant that their UEFA Cup place was awarded to Newcastle United, who were to play Inter Milan in the first round.

Chairman Sydney Bradley said, 'I am very disappointed, especially for the players. We shall have to do everything possible to remedy this for next season,' and Derby's mayor called it, 'a terrible injustice'.

Speculation, in the light of the decision, increased around the Manager's position, with Birmingham City leading the race offering a more stable club and big potential and bigger salaries. Birmingham Chairman Clifford Coombs made an official approach for their services at the beginning of May, as he tried to find a new Manager, having sacked Stan Cullis some six weeks previously.

Clough did little to kill off the speculation, by saying, 'Anyone could run this team for the next few years,' although the Chairman said, 'I see no reason to think that we shall lose them.'

Sam Longson took to the national press to highlight differences in the Boardroom that came to light as a result of the investigation, claiming that three Directors had not spoken to him for six months and he wanted them to resign. A couple of weeks later, Harry Payne (a Director since 1953), Vice-Chairman Ken Turner (due shortly to become Chairman) and Bob Kirkland were gone, and during the close season, three new Directors were appointed – Bob Innes, Bill Rudd and Michael Keeling. Longson himself took over as Chairman once again, and removed the stipulation that the term of office should only be for a two-year period. The new Directors were immediately responsible for a new organisation, Derby County Promotions, that was set up to bring all fundraising activities under one umbrella, and was directly controlled by the Club. Stuart Crooks, who was Secretary of the Supporters' Association, moved to be promotions organiser for the new department.

Stuart Webb was appointed as Secretary on 1st June 1970, arriving from Preston North End, where he had been Assistant Secretary for the previous eight years. Having had three secretaries during the previous three years, it was hoped that this appointment would bring some order to the administrative chaos that had ensued during the previous few years. The appointment was made without consulting Chairman Longson, who was somewhat annoyed as the role of Club Secretary was pivotal in light of the previous year's shortcomings.

August 1970

Football's first sponsored tournament, the Watney Mann Invitation Cup, was introduced in the pre-season of 1970. The participating teams were those that had scored the most goals in each of the four divisions of the Football League during the previous season who had not been promoted or admitted to one of the European competitions. Two teams from each division took part (Derby, Manchester United, Hull City, Sheffield United, Reading, Fulham, Aldershot and Peterborough United) and there was also the prospect of a penalty shoot-out being used for the first time in England, should any game end in a draw. Each club taking part was to receive an equal share of gate receipts and TV revenue, as well as £4,000 just for entering the competition.

In the first round, Derby were drawn away to Fulham, and this was the first time that Derby had been in a match that required extra-time to be played, eventually winning 5–3 after being 1–3 down after just 14 minutes. It was a blisteringly hot day in London and Alan Durban collapsed on the team coach on the way back due to heat exhaustion, and he later commented that he was glad Wales had not qualified for the World Cup in Mexico. A 1–0 home win against Sheffield United set up a Final against a Manchester United team that included George Best, Dennis Law, Bobby Charlton, et cetera. It was a one-way contest with a comfortable 4–1 win for The Rams in front of 32,000 fans.

The large trophy was presented to Dave Mackay by the FIFA President, Sir Stanley Rous.

Thursday 13ᵗʰ August 1970

Minute 6311 Manager's Report

Mr Peter Taylor, the Assistant Manager was called into the meeting and submitted the following report.

A specialist's report on Terry Hennessey's injury had shown no serious complications and the player would commence training immediately.

Arthur Stewart had been transferred to Ballymena United FC, for a fee of £1,000.

John Sims, an apprentice professional, had been signed full-time professional, at £18 per week.

The Chairman, on behalf of the Board of Directors, congratulated the Manager and Assistant Manager on the team's performance in winning the Watney Mann Invitation Cup.

Minute 6312 Watney Mann Cup – Financial Statement

The Secretary outlined the financial details regarding the Watney Mann competition. The club had made a profit of £13,910 before deduction of players' bonuses.

It was agreed that Manager and Assistant Manager receive a bonus of £250 each in respect of the club winning the competition.

The Chairman reported on letters of appreciation received fron Sir Stanley Rous, the Football League, and Watney Mann Limited, in respect of the organisation and hospitalities shown by the club during the competition.

A vote of thanks to the Secretary for his efforts in connection with match arrangements was proposed by Mr T. W. Rudd and seconded by Mr Walters.

A total donation of £250 was agreed to be distributed to local charities out of the match proceeds.

The Secretary is to prepare a list in accordance with previous years.

Minute 6314 Season ticket Sales 1970–71

The Secretary reported that Season ticket sales stood at £123,100 to date for the coming season.

Minute 6315 Insurance

Mr F. W. Innes reported that all parts of the ground and stands were now adequately covered and the Watney Mann Cup had also been insured.

Minute 6316 Football Association – Ground Safety

Further instructions regarding Ground and Structure Safety had been received from the Football Association. A complete report had to be submitted to the Football Association by 1st October 1970, signed by the relevant responsible bodies. It was agreed that Mr F. W. Innes and the Secretary make the necessary arrangements on behalf of the club.

Minute 6317 Un-Issued Share Capital

Mr T. W. Rudd reported that discussions had taken place with Bass Charrington in respect of proposed reissue of the undistributed Share Capital. The Brewery requested a full list of Directors' and Shareholders' holdings in the Company before committing themselves further. It was agreed the Secretary make the necessary arrangements.

Minute 6318 Derby County Promotions

Mr M. Keeling reported that £6,000 had been transferred to the Club's account from Derby County Promotions.

Mr S. Crooks, Draw Organiser Salary: £30 per week, plus car and petrol. Commission: Commission on all activities as follows: 5% on all profits over net receipts of £600 per week.

Minute 6319 Football Association – Fine

It was agreed to forward the £10,000 owing to the Football Association in respect of the fine imposed on the club.

Minute 6320 BBC TV

It was reported that BBC would be covering our home game with Burnley on Saturday 19th September 1970. Under the new agreement the club would receive £700.

Minute 6324 Bonuses – Manager & Assistant Manager

The following bonuses in respect of season 1969–70 were confirmed:

£5,000 – Manager, B. H. Clough

£5,000 – Assistant Manager, P. Taylor

The figures outstanding to date:

£4,000 to B. H. Clough

£2,000 to P. Taylor

Incentives agreed upon for 1970–71 season:

1st in Football League Division 1   £5,000 each

2nd in Football League Division 1   £2,500 each

3rd–4th–5th in Football League Division 1 £2,000 each

6th in Football League Division 1   £1,000 each

FA Cup

£500 each for reaching the Sixth Round.

£1,500 each for reaching the Semi-final.

£3,000 each for reaching the Cup Final.

Football League Cup

£1,000 each for reaching Semi-final (£1,000 each leg, per person).

£3,000 each for reaching the Cup Final.

Europe

£1,000 each if the Club qualifies for Europe.

Editor's Comments

Arthur Stewart, who had been at the Club since the arrival of Clough, was transferred back to his native Northern Ireland after making 30 appearances and scoring once. He went on to have a lengthy career upon his return and played for Distillery, Bangor, Cliftonville and Glentoran and was voted Ulster Player of the Year for the 1973–74 season.

The highlights of the Watney Cup Final were broadcast on ITV on their *Star Soccer* programme on the Sunday afternoon, generating more income for the clubs and raising the profile of the sponsor.

Terry Hennessey, the Welsh international captain, who had been signed from rivals Nottingham Forest during the previous season and had been struggling with a persistent knee injury, was set to miss the start of the season.

On the eve of the Football League season, Clough said, 'We intend being up with Leeds and Everton this season. I want to be top of the table when we meet Leeds in October.'

Friday 21ˢᵗ August 1970

Minute 6319 Manager's Report

The Manager reported that Roy McFarland had requested an increase in salary. It was agreed to pay McFarland £100 per week.

It was agreed to play the club's home Football League Cup Second Round fixture with Halifax Town on Tuesday 8th September 1970, subject to Football League permission.

On behalf of the Board of Directors, the Chairman expressed congratulations to the Manager in respect of the team's fine performance in beating Wolverhampton Wanderers 4–2 at the midweek fixture.

Minute 6323 Football Association – Ground & Spectator Safety

It was reported that a meeting with the local authority Inspectors – Police, Fire and Engineers Department would take place within the next ten days. Mr F. W. Innes and the Secretary would meet the visiting officials.

Minute 6324 Insurance

Mr F. W. Innes reported on Insurance matters, and it was agreed that cover be taken out in respect of ground damage following hooliganism.

Minute 6326 Derby County Promotions

Mr M. Keeling reported that arrangements were now completed in respect of launching this new venture, and it was agreed that a new account be opened with the National Westminster Bank Limited, Irongate, as from the 1st September 1970. It was also reported that two new shop assistants had commenced work at the club shop this week.

Minute 6327 Season tickets

The Secretary reported that Season ticket sales to date stood at £124,500 in respect of 1970–71.

Minute 6329 Midland's Sports Centre

Mr F. W. Innes reported that the proposed Sports Centre for the Midlands would not be in the form of a stadium, and therefore not of interest to Derby County Football Club.

Minute 6330 Ley Stand

It was agreed that enquiries be made in respect of proposed side partitions for the Ley Stand which have not been fitted.

Minute 6331 Administration

The Secretary outlined details of future reorganisation within the administrative side of the Company.

Thursday 27*th* August 1970

Minute 6335 Manager's Report

The Manager reported that Terry Hennessey was seeing a specialist today (27 August 1970) with suspected cartilage trouble.

Professional player, Pat Wright, had been granted a free transfer from the club.

Discussion took place regarding a further loan to player Les Green. It was left to Mr Clough to finalise the details.

It was reported that Gordon Guthrie, Second Team Trainer, had received a salary increase of £3 per week, up to £28 per week, to be backdated from 1st July 1970.

It was agreed that an estate car be purchased for club use, and the Chairman would look into the position regarding the First Team Trainer, Jimmy Gordon, and the new vehicle.

It was agreed that Mr B. H. Clough's salary would be increased to £7000 per annum and that expenses of £250 per annum would also be paid.

Minute 6338 Derby County Promotions

It was reported that an account had been opened with National Westminster Bank in respect of the new venture. The Chairman outlined that preliminary enquiries had been made in respect of a property for sale opposite the ground, in Shaftesbury Crescent, with a view to a selling point on match days.

Minute 6339 Proposed New Osmaston Stand

The Chairman confirmed that a meeting would take place at the Baseball Ground on Thursday 10th September 1970 at 12:00 noon with Banbury Grandstands Limited, in respect of the proposed Osmaston Stand.

Minute 6340 R. McFarland – Wages & Football League

The Secretary confirmed that the new contract given to Roy McFarland had been accepted by the Football League.

Minute 6341 Assistant Secretary

The Chairman outlined proposals for an appointment of Assistant Secretary.

Minute 6343 Official Programme

Discussion took place regarding the club's new programme, and the Chairman undertook to speak to the Programme Editor, Mr D. Moore, on the points raised by the Board of Directors.

Editor's Comments

Terry Hennessey had collapsed in the game against Stoke City and had been carried off, and would only last for 14 minutes in a reserve match, prompting a more detailed medical examination.

Pat Wright had played over 200 games for Shrewsbury Town in the five years before joining Derby in 1967. In the three years since then he had made just 13 appearances for the Club, all in the 1967–68 season, and was on loan at Southend United during 1970 making 11 appearances. After leaving Derby he signed for Rotherham United.

The midweek match against Coventry City was also a landmark event – it was the first time closed-circuit TV had been installed and used to cover the crowd looking out for potential troublemakers, now seen in every football stadium. The cameras were looking at areas behind the goals and the Popside as the most likely places where trouble would occur. Chief Superintendent Harry Shelley said, 'We pioneered the use of high-powered binoculars to detect troublemakers; we were the first to confiscate "bovver boots" and braces; and we were the first to have our own mini-police station inside a football ground.'

Thursday 10th September 1970

Minute 6345 Manager's Report

The Manager was called into the meeting to present his report on players, teams and any other relevant matters for the past week.

It was confirmed that a Ford Escort Estate car had been purchased for £835 and the vehicle would be used by Trainer/Coach Jimmy Gordon for club business.

It was agreed that a donation of £25 be forwarded to Tollerton Football Club in respect of a junior player, Phil Boyer, signed by Derby County some years ago.

Minute 6348 Assistant Secretary

It was confirmed that Mr J. Howarth had been appointed Assistant Secretary at £1,800 per annum and would commence his duties on Monday 14th September 1970.

Minute 6349 P. Thorpe – Wedding Present

It was agreed that a Crown Derby tea service, valued at £25, be presented to Clerical Assistant P. Thorpe, as a wedding present from the club.

Minute 6355 Mr F. W. Innes

On behalf of Mrs Innes and himself, Mr F. W. Innes thanked the Chairman and Directors for their kind present in respect of their Silver Wedding Anniversary.

Minute 6356 Lighting – Popular Side

It was agreed to meet a request from the Police in respect of light sockets under the Popular Side, to assist the closed-circuit television cameras at present being used on crowd control exercise at the ground.

Editor's Comments

Phil Boyer was a former trainee and signed professionally in November 1966, but was allowed to leave without making a single appearance. He has a unique distinction in making over 100 appearances for four different League clubs – York City, Bournemouth, Norwich City and Southampton, and scored over 150 goals and made one full appearance for the England national team.

Roy McFarland was ruled out of the Halifax Town League Cup tie with a hamstring injury, which would also keep him out of the Football League representative team to play the Irish League.

With recent home losses to Newcastle United and Southampton, the Manager was coming under some pressure to make some signings to fill in the gaps in the squad that was suffering due to injuries, but the Manager acknowledged that he was well aware of the dangers of operating with a small squad but did not want to buy players who would not be first choice with a fully fit squad available.

It was reported by the *Daily Express* that West Bromwich Albion were close to agreeing a deal for the transfer of Sunderland's Colin Todd for £150,000, with Todd submitting a transfer request and Sunderland in some financial difficulty.

On 12th September, Ken Blair played twice on the same day; in a 2–0 win against Nottingham Forest in the Midland Intermediate Cup in the morning and again later for the Reserves in a 3–2 win against Manchester United. Apprentice Peter Phelan did the same, but was a substitute in the afternoon game, in which he later scored.

Thursday 24th September 1970

Minute 6358 Manager's Report

The Manager reported that Terry Hennessey, Roy McFarland and Ron Webster would not be fit for the match with West Bromwich Albion on Saturday 26th September 1970.

It was agreed to grant Ron Webster a Testimonial game towards the end of the season in recognition of ten years' service with the club. Permission to stage the game at the Baseball Ground was granted subject to Football League approval.

The Manager confirmed that a Derby County eleven would play at Peterborough United on Monday 12th October 1970 in aid of Eddie Holliday's testimonial.

It was agreed to allow Top Ten Eleven Promotions to stage a testimonial game for Jackie Stamps at the Baseball Ground on Monday12th October 1970 subject to Football League permission. The Top Ten eleven would probably play a Burton Albion eleven.

Minute 6359 Archie Gemmill

The transfer of registration of Archie Gemmill from Preston North End to Derby County for £59,000 (fifty nine thousand pounds) was confirmed. Details of payment to Preston North End as follows:

First payment	£30,000
By 30th November 1970	£9,000
By 31st December 1970	£5,000
By 31st January 1971	£5,000
By 28th February 1971	£5,000
By 30th April 1971	**£5,000**
	£59,000

A. Gemmill to receive basic wage of £80 per week and 5% of the transfer fee: £3,245 as follows:

> £1,622.10.0 on or before 30th June 1971
>
> £1,622.10.0 on or before 30th June 1972

Minute 6362 Football League Cup Third Round v. Millwall

The Secretary outlined proposals for ticket distribution for the Third Round Football League Cup tie v. Millwall on Wednesday 7th October 1970.

Minute 6363 Derby County Promotions

It was reported that £5,000 had been transferred to the club account from Derby County Promotions.

Minute 6365 Proposed Osmaston Stand

Discussion took place regarding the proposed New Osmaston Stand and Mr S. C. Bradley outlined the up-to-date position regarding Ley's Malleable Castings Company Limited and the club's proposals.

Minute 6366 Television at the Baseball Ground

It was confirmed that the Club's home game v. Tottenham Hotspur on Saturday 3rd October 1970 would be televised by ITV and that the home game v. Leeds United on 24th October 1970 would be covered by the BBC.

Minute 6368 Share Capital Re-Issue

Mr T. W. Rudd confirmed that negotiations with Bass Charrington Brewery were well in hand and a full analysis of the situation would be prepared according to the Brewery's attitude towards the Board's proposals.

Thursday 1ˢᵗ October 1970

Minute 6370 Assistant Manager's Report

Mr Peter Taylor, Assistant Manager, came into the meeting and reported on Club affairs generally.

It was reported that Graham Chadwick, an apprentice professional with the Club, had had his contract terminated by mutual consent and had returned home to the North East.

It was confirmed that John Robson had been selected to play for England Under-23s v. West Germany at Leicester on Wednesday 14th October 1970. Two official invitations had been received for Directors to attend the official reception.

Minute 6375 Sinfin Sports Ground

Mr F. W. Innes reported that might the Club be interested in selling Sinfin Sports Ground, a figure of £150,000 would be obtainable for this valuable site on present-day values. The Chairman undertook to speak to the Manager, Mr B. H. Clough, on the matter and look into all aspects of a possible sale.

Minute 6376 Draft Accounts 1969-70

A copy of the Draft Accounts regarding the financial year ended 31st July 1970 were handed to members of the Board. The Chairman outlined that a modern presentation of accounts would be drafted out by the Secretary, together with the Club Accountant, Mr Mason, and be presented to the Board at the next meeting.

It was also agreed to bring the Annual General Meeting forward to the last week of November 1970.

Thursday 15th October 1970

Minute 6378 Manager's Report

The Manager reported on the present injury position and that Terry Hennessey would be extremely doubtful for Saturday's home game versus Chelsea.

Anthony Rhodes, reserve team centre-half, was available for transfer and clubs in the Second, Third and Fourth Divisions had been notified.

Minute 6380 Draft Accounts

It was agreed to adopt draft accounts for year ending 31st July 1970 as submitted. The Chairman and Secretary undertook to see Mr Forsyth – Auditor and express the Board of Directors decision that the Company would be reappointing Forsyth's as Auditors following the Annual General Meeting.

Minute 6384 GEC Floodlighting Demonstration

It was agreed that members of the Board would attend a floodlighting demonstration at the Baseball Ground that evening, arranged by GEC.

Editor's Comments

Kevin Hector and John Robson had played for the Football League against the Irish Football League at Carrow Road, Norwich, with Hector scoring the last goal in a comfortable 5–0 win.

During the week, Derby had made an offer regarding the possible transfer of the Nottingham Forest midfielder and captain, Henry Newton, for a fee of around £150,000. Liverpool, West Ham United, Arsenal and Everton were also aiming to acquire his signature, with Everton leading the chase with a cash offer plus a player moving in the opposite direction, which was thought to be favoured by the Nottingham club. Clough said after the deal had been concluded, 'this is a great disappointment since we had been after Henry for eighteen months. We would have had to almost mortgage the stand but we would have done that for Newton.'

Colin Todd, the Sunderland and England Under-23 captain, had given in another transfer request to his club, fearing that his career would suffer if he was to stay in the Second Division for any length of time. Manchester United were waiting to make a six-figure offer as soon as the North-East club had found a suitable defensive replacement.

It was now five weeks since Terry Hennessey's cartilage operation and reports were suggesting that he was making good progress.

The special supporters' train that had been running for a few years was finally given a name, thanks to a recent competition held via the match programme. PC John Dunford, actually Assistant Secretary Michael Dunford's father, was chosen as the winner with his entry of 'Ramaway' being chosen. The first official excursion to go under the Ramaway banner was the trip to Everton.

Thursday 29ᵗʰ October 1970

Minute 6389 Manager's Report

The Manager was called into the meeting to report on relevant matters for the past week.

Willie Carlin had been transferred to Leicester City for a gross fee of £38,888, Derby County to receive £35,000 net.

Minute 6390 Jack Stamps – Testimonial

The Secretary gave a financial report on the Jack Stamps Testimonial match. After all expenses, the Net cash amounted to £4,325. It was agreed that in the absence of the Chairman, Sir Robertson King KBE would present the cheque to J. Stamps prior to the Liverpool game on Saturday 7ᵗʰ November 1970.

Minute 6392 Sinfin Sports Ground

It was agreed that Mr F. W. Innes on behalf of the Company make provisional enquiries in respect of planning permission for Sinfin to be converted into a shopping precinct. This would enable the Club to place a realistic value on the site.

Minute 6393 Draft Accounts & Annual General Meeting

The Secretary outlined the new form of Company Balance Sheet, which was confirmed. Notice of meeting and agendas would be posted to shareholders on Tuesday 10th November 1970. The Annual General Meeting would be held on Friday 4th December 1970, in the Boardroom at 10.30 a.m.

It was confirmed that Auditor A. Neil Forsyth was to retire as Auditor of the Company at the meeting. His letter of resignation was accepted and it was agreed that for past services, a presentation be made to Mr Forsyth from the Company.

Minute 6394 Derby County Promotions

Mr M. Keeling confirmed that a further £5,000 had been transferred to the Club's account from Derby County Promotions.

Minute 6396 Texaco

Discussion took place regarding the contract for ground advertising taken out for three years with Texaco. It was agreed that some minor details regarding dates and International games to be played at Derby be ironed out before completion. Mr Rudd and the Secretary undertook to finalise the contract and present the facts at the next meeting.

Editor's Comments

Willie Carlin had made just one appearance for his hometown club Liverpool before moving to Halifax Town, Carlisle United and Sheffield United, before signing for Derby and playing a pivotal role in their rise from Division Two to the upper reaches of Division One. After leaving Leicester, he also played for Notts County and Cardiff City.

On the field, things were not going so well, recording just one win in the League since August (10 games) and that was against the bottom club Burnley. With the exception of Gemmill replacing Carlin, this was the same group of players that had performed so well during the previous season and lack of form was as much as anything down to confidence. A break to Majorca prior to the Liverpool game was to clear the air and refocus the players.

On 7th November, goalkeeper Les Green made his 100th consecutive appearance in the game against Liverpool, having missed just one game since signing for the club at the start of the 1968–69 season.

Members of the team set off for the BBC TV studios in Birmingham on 9th November to record their first-round game in a new TV show called *Quiz Ball* (v. Cowdenbeath) where various lighted routes to goal matched the question difficulty. One of which was Route 1, which made its way into the media as a generic term for direct football.

Thursday 19th November 1970

Minute 6399 Manager's Report

The Manager was called into the meeting to report on relevant matters for the past week.

It was confirmed that Anthony Rhodes had been transferred to Halifax Town for a net fee of £3,500, to be paid as follows:

£1,000	down payment
£400	by 1st January 1971
£400	by 1st February 1971
£400	by 1st March 1971
£400	by 1st April 1971
£400	by 1st May 1971
£400	by 1st June 1971
£400	by 1st July 1971

It was agreed that for the Central League game with Nottingham Forest on Wednesday 25th November 1970, the Ley Stand be open to the public at 3 shillings per person.

Minute 6400 Sinfin Sports Ground

Mr F. W. Innes, on behalf of the Board, would be looking into the possibility of obtaining an alternative site, should the Club sell Sinfin. The Manager and Assistant Manager would assist with the enquiries.

Minute 6404 Vulcan Street Car Park Wall

A request for the wall adjoining the Vulcan Street Car Park to be repaired had been received from a resident of Harrington Street. After discussion, it was agreed that Mr T. W. Rudd would look into the matter on behalf of the Company.

Minute 6407 Texaco

The Secretary reported that the contract for ground advertising with Texaco would be completed within the next few days.

Editor's Comments

Tony Rhodes had only made a handful of first team matches before his transfer and he went on to have a long career at Halifax Town, making over 230 appearances for the Yorkshire club.

Roy McFarland had been named in the full England squad to face East Germany at Wembley on 25th November, with only John Sadler of Manchester United in his way. However, he picked up an injury that saw him in hospital with his leg immobilised and lost the opportunity for his first full cap, and also had to withdraw from the England Under-23 match against Wales on 2nd December.

On the same night, the Reserves match against Nottingham Forest had been brought forward from Saturday as the first team was to meet the same opponents at the City Ground. The Reserves were in good form, being unbeaten in 11 games and winning 8 in a row, and made it 9 in a row by winning 4–1 in front of 7,500 fans and prompting possible further Reserve fixtures to be played during the week.

On 1st December, the *Quiz Ball* team defeated Tottenham Hotspur 3–2 in the semi-final of the televised competition.

German giants Bayern Munich had wanted to bring their stars including Franz Beckenbauer, Gerd Muller, et cetera to the Baseball Ground for a friendly, but the FA had refused permission due to the existing one-year ban from playing foreign opposition anywhere imposed on the club at the start of the season.

Alan Hinton had broken a bone in his right foot and would be out of action for three weeks.

Birmingham City, in the lower reaches of the Second Division, had made an enquiry about Dave Mackay, currently out injured with a dislocated finger, and Burnley, Blackpool and Bolton Wanderers were also interested. After a meeting between Clough and Mackay on 25th November, Clough said, 'It's pointless Birmingham City or any other clubs making inquiries. We are not letting him go.'

Thursday 3rd December 1970

Minute 6409 Manager's Report

The Manager reported on the present injury situation and outlined details of the team to meet West Ham United.

The following games at the Baseball Ground were confirmed:

Monday 7th December 1970

Youth Cup Replay Derby County v. Aston Villa

Tuesday 8th December 1970

Central League Derby County v. Coventry City

Monday 14th December 1970

Representative game, Derby County v. British Olympic XI

Minute 6410 Annual General Meeting

The Secretary outlined final arrangements for the Company's Annual General Meeting to be held at the Baseball Ground on Friday, 4th December 1970. No nominations had been received in respect of applications for seats on the Board.

Minute 6411 Texaco

Details of the contract for ground, ticket and programme advertising with Texaco Limited were confirmed:

£12,000 for the remainder of Season 1970–71.

£12,000 for Season 1971–72 and an option for a further £12,000 in respect of 1972–73, subject to agreement between both parties.

A further £2,000 per season should Derby County qualify for a European competition.

Should any representative game be staged at the Baseball Ground, a sum would be negotiable on a match to match agreement.

Texaco would also paint parts of the Baseball Ground when incorporating their advertising boards, subject to approval.

A vote of thanks from the Chairman and Board of Directors was extended to Director Mr M. Keeling and Secretary Mr A. S. Webb for their efforts in respect of the organising and negotiating of the contract.

Minute 6414 Share Capital

Mr T. W. Rudd confirmed that Bass Worthington (Midlands) Limited would be in favour of Derby County increasing its authorised Share Capital to £100,000 should the Company decide to issue more shares.

Discussion took place regarding the possibilities of introducing new capital, and also tidying up the Share Register in general. It was agreed that proposals would be submitted to the Board in the new year, and for the moment, Mr T. W. Rudd and the Secretary would formulate the necessary information.

Editor's Comments

On 5th December, Dave Mackay made his 100th appearance for the club since joining in the summer of 1968, in a 2–4 home defeat to West Ham United. Manager Clough missed the game as he was on a scouting mission at the Notts County v. Bournemouth game, but denied that he was interested in signing Bournemouth prolific scorer Ted MacDougall but was after 'players who can defend'.

Derby played a friendly against a British Olympic XI on the afternoon of 14th December. Derby's team that afternoon had a Gambian player on a one-month trial – his name was Alhaji Momodo Nije, better known as Biri Biri. Unfortunately, the trial did not work out for either party and he later went on to play for Spanish club Sevilla for five years, becoming a fans' favourite, and he is regarded as Gambia's greatest ever player.

Thursday 17th December 1970

Minute 6417 Assistant Manager's Report

Mr P. Taylor, Assistant Manager, reported on the injury position and the probable teams for Saturday.

It was agreed that a donation of £25 be forwarded to the Birkley Community Centre Football Club in respect of John Robson.

The following wage increases for members of the Training Staff were confirmed:

John Sheridan - £5 increase to £30 per week.

Gordon Guthrie - £2 increase to £30 per week.

Minute 6418 FA Cup Third Round v. Chester (away)

The Secretary outlined arrangements for distribution of tickets in respect of the all-ticket FA Cup game with Chester on Saturday 2nd January 1971.

Discussion took place regarding ticket arrangements for the Nottingham Forest game at the Baseball Ground on 30th January 1971, and after discussion, it was agreed that subject to agreement with Nottingham Forest and the Police, this game would not be all-ticket.

Minute 6419 Derby County Promotions

The Secretary confirmed a further donation of £5,000 from Derby County Promotions. Details of the Junior Rams Xmas Spectacular to take place at Tiffany's Ballroom on Monday 21st December 1970 were confirmed.

Thursday 31st December 1970

Minute 6422 Manager's Report

The Manager reported on the injury position and team selection news.

Discussion took place regarding player Les Green and his present financial difficulties. Mr P. Taylor, the Assistant Manager, was called into the meeting to elaborate on the position and, after discussion, it was agreed to leave the matter until the next Board Meeting.

Minute 6423 Ground Facilities

Discussion took place regarding the proposed new stand and, after a lengthy discussion, it was agreed that preliminary plans and drawings for a new stand at the Normanton End be prepared, but it would not be possible to commence this scheme during 1971.

It was, however, agreed that general ground amenities be improved during the coming close season and schemes in respect of refreshment bars for both 'B' Stand and Ley Stand were sanctioned. Plans of both schemes would be available for a future meeting.

Minute 6424 Derby County Promotions

The Secretary outlined details of the loan and joint promotional scheme that would operate from 1st February 1971 with Burton Albion Football Club. Report of the Junior Rams Xmas spectacular was also put to the meeting.

Minute 6425 Halifax Town

It was reported that Halifax Town were seven weeks outstanding in respect of the £1,000 down payment regarding A. Rhodes. A further £400 being due on 1st January 1971. The Secretary was instructed to inform Halifax Town that if the payment was not made within the next seven days, the matter would be placed before the Football League Management Committee.

Minute 6427 Fire Insurance

The Secretary outlined proposals for increased fire cover on all stands, in the form of 'Reinstatement', based on the Insurance Companies agreeing in advance, to pay 'new for old'. It was agreed that financial details in respect of additional cover be prepared and submitted to a subsequent meeting.

Editor's Comments

Derby's defence had conceded more goals up to this point in the season that the whole of the previous season, and Les Green was pinpointed as a possible cause of that as other teams had possibly worked out how to overcome that fact that he was the smallest goalkeeper in the Division, at just 5 ft 8 inches. After 127 consecutive appearances, he was replaced in goal for the FA Cup third-round match away to Chester City by Colin Boulton.

On 5th January, the final of the BBC TV show *Quiz Ball* was broadcast, with Derby winning the trophy by defeating Crystal Palace 4–2.

Thursday 21st January 1971

Manager's Report

The Manager reported on the injury position and team for the Fourth Round FA Cup game with Wolverhampton Wanderers. Terry Hennessey was still having trouble with his knee and a second opinion would be taken.

An invitation from the Football League to take part in the Anglo-Italian Club Competition during the summer was turned down. It was felt that the competition dates would not allow sufficient time for the proposed new seating and refreshment bars to be completed in time for the new season.

It was confirmed that the Reserve Team would play at Huddersfield on Tuesday 26th January 1971 in a rearranged Central League fixture.

Extraordinary General meeting

The Chairman outlined progress in respect of the proposed Extraordinary General Meeting. Mr Timms would be meeting the Chairman on Friday 22nd January 1971 with a proposed agenda. Mr F. W. Innes reported that a valuation of the Ground should be available within the next few days.

Season tickets 1971–72

The Secretary submitted proposals to the meeting in respect of Season tickets for season 1971–72. It was agreed to increase the price of Stand seats by 2/- all round. Ground and Paddock prices to be decided later when the views of the Football League and other clubs had been sought.

Season tickets would include four home Cup tie vouchers for which supporters would pay for in advance, i.e.:

	Per Match	Basic Season	21 Games	Saving	Four Vouchers	Total Cost of Season ticket	Cost to 25% non-voucher holders
Goal Stands	14/-	£13	£14.14.0	£1.14.0	£2.16.0	£15.16.0	£13
Wing Stands	16/-	£15	£16.16.0	£1.16.0	£3.4.0		
Centre Stands	20/-	£17	£21	£4	£4	£21	£17

a. All Season ticket holders to be written to personally along with programme and press announcements.

a. Present voucher holders will be allowed from 1st May – 21st May (3 weeks) to collect their own seats, complete with Cup Vouchers, for next season.

a.   Any unclaimed Cup Voucher seats after 21st May will be sold to present non-voucher holders. Non-voucher holders will receive first allowance of any proposed new seating under Osmaston Stand and will have Cup Vouchers included.

a.   The price of Season tickets for 1971–72 will include the first four home Cup ties played in, whether the Football League Cup or the Football Association Challenge Cup.

a.   If prices of admission are raised for any of these matches in FL Cup or FA Cup it means that Season ticket holders will not have to pay extra.

a.   For all home Cup ties, Season ticket holders need not apply for tickets, no queues or postal applications. New systems save time and effort all round.

a.   If fewer than four League Cup and FA Cup matches are played at home, then a CREDIT will be held over for the following season, or the cost refunded on application.

a.   If more than four League Cup and FA Cup matches are played at home, then the old system will operate for these matches (i.e. Sunday sale and postal applications).

Balance at Bank

The overdrawn balance to date on the Club's account stood at £30,000.

Mayor's Reception

It was agreed that the Club would attend a Mayoral Reception at the Town Hall on Monday 1st March 1971.

'B' Stand Refreshment Bar

It was agreed that Mr T. Gould be advised to process with plans and specifications in respect of Refreshment Bar for next season. A request for approximate cost to be included.

Editor's Comments

On the morning of the Wolverhampton Wanderers game, Peter Taylor was taken to hospital by Brian Clough complaining of chest pains. Further examinations found that he was showing the after-effects of a heart attack that had occurred sometime before (traced back to the Arsenal away game). As a result of this, he would be forced to have several weeks' complete rest at home, away from the pressures of the football club.

Attendances at the Baseball Ground had passed the half-million mark with 522,370 fans attending the 13 League, 2 League Cup and 2 Watney Cup games, at an average of 30,727.

Thursday 28th January 1971

Minute 6444 Manager's Report

The Manager was called into the meeting to report on relevant team matters during the past week and outline proposed teams for Saturday.

Archie Gemmill had been selected to travel with the Scottish FA party to Belgium for their Nations Cup Competition. It was agreed that a letter of congratulations from the Chairman and Board of Directors be sent to A. Gemmill in recognition of this, his first major honour.

It was reported that Terry Hennessey was to have a second cartilage operation on the same knee and would be out of action for approximately six to eight weeks.

Minute 6445 Share Capital Issue

It was confirmed that an Extraordinary General Meeting in respect of the unissued Share Capital would not be necessary.

It was proposed by Mr S. Longson, and seconded by Mr T. W. Rudd, and unanimously agreed that the 13,852 unissued shares in the company be offered to existing shareholders on a pro-rata basis on their present holding.

A valuation of £1.5.0 per share had been received from Mr Mason, the Club accountant, based on present day values.

The Company would appoint underwriters to cover the issue and the following five underwriters were confirmed:

A. Pinder   proposed by Mr S. Longson
C. Frost   proposed by Mr S. Longson
H. Porter   proposed by Mr S. C. Bradley
A. H. Gould   proposed by Mr T. W. Rudd
A. Harris   proposed by Mr M. Keeling

Minute 6447 Texaco

The Chairman reported that £12,000 in respect of season 1970–71 had been received from Texaco for ground advertising. A further £12,000 being due on 1st August 1971 for season 1971–72.

Minute 6448 FA Cup Fifth Round v. Everton (away) 13th February 1971

The Secretary outlined details of the ticket distribution in respect of the away Fifth Round Cup tie with Everton.

A vote of thanks to the Secretary and his staff was proposed by Sir Robertson King KBE and seconded by Mr T. W. Rudd in respect of the administrative organisation at the recent all-ticket Cup tie with Wolverhampton Wanderers at the Baseball Ground.

Minute 6449 Chairman

On behalf of the Board of Directors, Mr S. C. Bradley expressed all good wishes to Mr and Mrs Longson for their forthcoming holiday.

Minute 6551 Crystal Palace 17th February 1971

It was confirmed that due to FA Cup Fifth Round commitments, the Football League game with Crystal Palace due to be played on 13th February 1971 would now be played on Wednesday 17th February 1971, kick-off 7:30 p.m.

Thursday 11ᵗʰ February 1971

Minute 6553 Manager's Report

Mr B. H. Clough came into the meeting and reported that the team were at present in Majorca for a few days' special training prior to the Fifth Round Cup tie with Everton. Terry Hennessey had recovered from his operation and it was hoped that he would soon be fit to commence light training. Mr P. Taylor, the Assistant Manager, reported to the Board on his progress following his recent illness. The Chairman and Directors expressed good wishes to Mr Taylor for his continued recovery.

Discussion took place regarding the verbal report of the ground specialist from Bingley Research Laboratories on the state of the playing area. It was agreed that a comprehensive written report be made available for discussion when the Chairman returned from holiday.

Minute 6554 Share Capital Issue

The Secretary reported that following the Accountant's half yearly audit and his visit to see Mr Mason along with Mr F. W. Innes regarding the share valuation, a new report was to hand. Three separate share valuations had been made and had resulted as follows:

  a. Taken as a going concern at 31ˢᵗ January 1971 and including all Stands at cost less depreciation resulting in <u>approximately £6 per share.</u>
  b. Taken as a going concern but value of Stands and Ground included at a force sale valuation as prepared by Gerald Maynard & Co., resulting in a <u>Deficiency as to Capital.</u>
  c. Taking Gerald Maynard & Co., valuation of land only and adding written down Balance Sheet figures for Stands, Buildings at 31ˢᵗ January 1971 which results in an <u>approximate £27 to £28 per share</u>.

Minute 6556 Football League re. A. Gemmill v. Preston North End

The Secretary reported that he had attended the Football League Enquiry along with Gemmill. It resulted in Gemmill receiving a further £2,700 from Preston North End in respect of his transfer to Derby County last November.

Tuesday 23rd February 1971

Joint Meeting of Directors and Underwriters

In Connection with Proposed Issue of 13,852 Unissued Shares in the Company

PRESENT:

DIRECTORS	Mr S. C. Bradley
	Mr F. W. Walters
	Mr T. W. Rudd
	Mr F. W. Innes
UNDERWRITERS	Mr A. Finder
	Mr C. Frost
	Mr A. Harris
	Mr H. Porter
	Mr H. Timms
SECRETARY	Mr A. S. Webb

Mr Timms explained the duties and commitments that would be required by the Underwriters in an exercise of this nature. He also read the Ground and Land valuations prepared by Gerald Maynard & Co. which came to £65,000 for the Baseball Ground and £60,000 for Sinfin Lane Sports Ground.

A Report from H. R. Horne & Partners, Club Accountants, covering present day share valuations based on various theories was also read and explained to the Underwriters.

Following general discussion, it was proposed by the Underwriters that the

13,852 outstanding shares be offered at par (£1) to existing shareholders. It was agreed that this proposal from the Underwriters be submitted to the next Board of Directors for discussion.

On behalf of the Board of Directors, Mr S. C. Bradley thanked Mr Timms and the Underwriters for their attendance.

Monday 1st March 1971

Minute 6558 Manager's Report

The Manager, Mr B. H. Clough and Assistant Manager, Mr P. Taylor both came into the meeting and reported on general team matters and the circumstances leading up to the transfer from Sunderland to Derby County of Colin Todd.

The following financial details in respect of the transfer agreement were confirmed:

Gross amount of transfer	£175,000
5% to Football League	£8,750
5% to C. Todd in 4 instalments	**£8,750**
Net amount due to Sunderland	**£157,500**

Payable as follows:

£80,000	by 1st March 1971
£40,000	by 30th June 1971
£37,500	**by 31st July 1971**
£157,000	

Discussion took place regarding reconstruction of the playing surface. It was agreed that a complete restart was not necessary and that minor work would be undertaken during the close season at an approximate cost of between £2,000 and £3,000.

Minute 6559 Share Capital Issue

Following the meeting of Underwriters and their proposals to underwrite the issue at £1 per share, it was agreed that this sum of £1 was under value. After a lengthy discussion it was proposed by Mr T. W. Rudd, seconded by Mr M. Keeling and agreed that a figure of £2 each be placed on the Shares.

Minute 6560 Balance at Bank

With the initial payment of £80,000 to Sunderland and Todd having been paid, it was confirmed that the overdrawn balance on the Company's account stood at £105,000.

Minute 6561 ATV v. Manchester City

It was confirmed that ATV would televise the home game v. Manchester City on Saturday 13th March 1971.

Minute 6562 Season tickets 1971–72

The Secretary outlined revised details of Season ticket prices and distribution. All Stand Season ticket holders would receive a letter with complete details of the process at the next home game against Manchester City. Tickets would go on sale on Monday 26th April 1971.

Minute 6563 Mr A. S. Webb

It was agreed that the Secretary's salary be increased by an additional £1,000 per annum from 1st March 1971.

Editor's Comments

The signing of Colin Todd saw one of the first public appearances of Peter Taylor following his heart attack, and pictures of him at the signing showed him looking thin with a beard, pipe and leather jacket.

It is possible to trace back the eventual fall-out between Clough and the Board to this signing, as although Chairman Longson agreed in principle to the signing, he had no idea of the magnitude of it. Whether by accident or design, the Chairman was on holiday in Antigua, West Indies and was unaware of the £175,000 fee until the Coventry City Chairman, Derrick Robbins and Crystal Palace Chairman, Arthur Waite told him over dinner one evening. Clough did send a telegram to the Chairman – 'Signed you another good player, Todd. Running short of cash.'

Longson said in the autobiography *Sam's Story*, published in 2013, '... to spend that kind of money without consultation could have put the club into serious financial difficulties. I was perturbed to say the least. I don't think the relationship between Brian and myself, once so seemingly untarnishable, was ever quite the same again.'

In his programme notes in the Arsenal match programme, Clough said, 'The fee that we have paid is a huge amount of money, but it comes out of earned income plus (and this is a reasonable gamble, I think) Season ticket sales during the summer.' Clough was not aware that the club was already £25,000 overdrawn at the Bank before the first £80,000 instalment for Todd's transfer was taken out.

Todd himself was just 22 years old, and was the current captain of the Sunderland and England Under-23 teams, where he had won 10 caps to date. He had known Clough beforehand as a 15-year-old when he was in charge of the Sunderland youth team whilst Todd was there.

Peter Taylor commented during the press conference on the Friday morning that, 'I have seen nobody who can win the ball better than this lad. He also possesses composure, which all great sides need.' The fee itself was the second largest transfer (£200,000 for Martin Peters between West Ham United and Tottenham Hotspur) and the 27th over £100,000.

During the week following his transfer, on Wednesday 24th February, Todd (as captain) and John Robson played for the England Under-23 team against Scotland, and 15-year-old Steve Powell, who was attached to Derby on schoolboy forms, was captain of the England Schoolboy team against their Northern Irish counterparts at Wembley Stadium on 6th March.

As the Baseball Ground pitch began to deteriorate during the winter months, various experts often dropped by to see groundsman Bob Smith and the latest one was Walter Goodyear, groundsman at Derbyshire County Cricket Club, who had recently won cricket's Groundsman of the Year.

Friday 12th March 1971

Minute 6565 Manager's Report

Mr B. H. Clough, the Manager, reported on the club's injury position and announced teams for Saturday's fixtures. Outgoing transfer negotiations prior to the deadline on March 11th had been promising with the possibility of Frank Wignall going to Leicester City and Barry Butlin to Preston North End. Neither of those, however, finally materialised.

It was confirmed that new signing Colin Todd had signed a two-year contract at £5,000 per annum with the usual incentives.

It was confirmed that Roy McFarland would represent the Football League v. Scottish League on Wednesday 17th March 1971 in Glasgow.

Minute 6566 Season tickets 1971–72

The Secretary confirmed prices and procedure in respect of Season ticket process for Stands in respect of 1971–72 season.

Minute 6567 National Westminster Bank Limited

The Chairman confirmed the financial arrangements with the Bank in respect of the transfer fee outstanding to Sunderland in respect of Todd. Temporary limit increased to £110,000 until end of April, to be reduced to £95,000 by the end of May, by when it can be anticipated to be within the original limit of £30,000. The full annual review of the Club's requirements would take place in July when the position for 1971–72 could be looked at in more detail.

Minute 6568 Share Capital Issue

A progress report on the Share Capital Issue confirmed that all documents connected with the issue were with council for final opinion and should be returned within the next week.

Minute 6569 Balance at Bank

The overdrawn balance on the Club's account to date stood at £110,700.

Minute 6572 Proposed New Club Room

Prices and specifications in respect of the proposed new refreshment room and toilets under 'B' Stand were discussed. It was agreed that a price of £19,706 by F. Dyson & Sons Limited of Huddersfield be accepted. Work would commence March/April in order to complete for commencement of season 1971–72. Bass Charrington would be invited to assist with this project along with a catering company.

Minute 6573 Ground Safety – Police Liaison

It was confirmed that the Chairman and Secretary would attend a meeting with local police on Wednesday 24th March 1971 in respect of Ground Safety.

Minute 6574 Mr Haines

It was confirmed that the Board of Directors would meet Mr Haines of Mobsby, Haines & Co Ltd following the next Board Meeting to discuss Mr Haines meeting with Derby Corporation in respect of major ground improvements.

Editor's Comments

Roy McFarland was selected to play for the Football League against the Scottish League on March 17th.

It was announced that next season's Season tickets would include four pre-paid Cup vouchers, initially to all existing 12,000 seat Season ticket holders. This was a major innovation as it would save time, trouble and expense for all concerned for the first four home Cup matches. Stuart Webb explained that if there were not four home matches, then the financial balance could be used as a credit against the following Season ticket or refunded to the supporter. If there were more than four matches, then the proven, existing system of Sunday and postal sales would remain.

A testimonial match for long-serving defender Ron Webster had been approved and the match against Coventry City would take place on 24th March with seat tickets costing 50p seats, and 30p on the terraces.

The Reserves game against leaders Liverpool was brought forward to the Friday night to give as many fans as possible the chance to see the game. Otherwise the attendance would have been diminished, as the game would take place on the Saturday afternoon at the same time as the first team fixture.

Thursday 25th March 1971

Minute 6576 Manager's Report

Mr B. H. Clough reported on relevant team matters and the Club's present injury position.

Minute 6577 Season tickets 1971–72

The Secretary reported that the circular letter to all Stand Season ticket Holders has been generally well received. It was agreed to fix prices for Ground and Popular Side at a later meeting. The new seating under Osmaston Stand would also be discussed at a later date when the position and demand could be assessed.

Minute 6578 Police

The Chairman reported on a meeting with the Police authorities in respect of Ground and Crowd control which had been attended by himself, Mr M. Keeling and the Secretary.

Minute 6579 Derby County Promotions

The Secretary reported that a further donation of £5,000 had been credited to the Club's account. Discussion took place regarding a new programme image for next season. It was proposed by Mr M. Keeling and agreed that the matter by thoroughly investigated and a report made to the next meeting on the subject of a club newssheet.

Minute 6580 Balance at Bank

The overdrawn balance on the Company's account was £105,000 to date.

Friday 4ᵗʰ April 1971

Minute 6583 Manager's Report

Mr B. H. Clough, the Manager, reported on the Club's injury position and announced probable teams for the Easter period.

It was reported that Les Green was still in financial difficulties and the Manger informed the Board of Directors that he advised no further financial assistance be given to Green.

Minute 6584 Season tickets 1971–72

It was agreed to leave Ground Season tickets at £5 and £6 respectively for the coming season and to include the Cup Vouchers.

Complete list of prices:

	With Cup Vouchers	League Game Only
'B' Stand & Ley Centre	£21	£17
'A' & 'C' Stands & Ley Wings	£17.20	£14
Osmaston & Normanton Stand	£14.80	£12
Normanton & Osmaston Terracing	£7.60	
Paddock (Shaftesbury Crescent)	£7.60	
Popular Side	£6.20	
Children's Pen	£3.60	

Discussion took place regarding additional seats under Osmaston Stand and it was agreed that a decision be taken at the next meeting when estimates of the cost would be available.

Minute 6586 Vulcan St Car Park

Following complaints and damage to vehicles in the Vulcan Street Car Park it was agreed that a suitable fence be erected around the area as soon as possible.

The Chairman reported on the progress made by Mr Timms in respect of the Share Issue.

Thursday 22nd April 1971

Minute 6588 Manager's Report

Mr B. H. Clough, the Manager, reported on relevant team matters. It was reported that Dave Mackay would sign for Swindon Town on 1st May 1971 following the final game v. West Bromwich Albion. A fee of £20,000 had been agreed, breakdown as follows:

Gross Fee	£20,000		
Payable	£9,000 by 15th June 1971	5% to League	£1,000
	£9,000 by 15th July 1971	5% to player	£1,000
	£18,000 Net fee to Derby County		

A request for a testimonial game had been turned down by the Football League but it was agreed to present a piece of Royal Crown Derby to Mackay following the game for services to the Club.

A vote of thanks to the Chairman and Manager for this transfer was expressed by members of the Board.

The team would take part in a 10-day tour of Majorca directly following the end of the season. Leaving Derby on Tuesday 4th May 1971, playing Real Mallorca on Wednesday 5th May 1971. The three senior officials travelling were Director in charge, Mr M. Keeling, Secretary Mr S. Webb and Assistant Manager, Mr P. Taylor.

Minute 6590 Derby County Promotions

The Secretary reported that a further donation of £5,000 had been handed over to the Club's account. The total to date for the year being £80,000.

Minute 6591 Proposed New Seats, Osmaston Stand

A verbal quotation by Messrs Perks of £11,250 was accepted. The scheme would give an additional 1,600 seats but would bring the overall ground capacity down to 40,500. It was agreed that an announcement be made by the Secretary to the press towards the end of May, when the majority of Stand Season tickets had been sold.

Minute 6592 Alan Hill Testimonial Fund

It was agreed that a donation of £10 be made to the testimonial fund of the late Nottingham Forest goalkeeper.

Minute 6593 ATV Derby County v. West Bromwich Albion

It was reported that the last home game v. West Bromwich Albion would be televised by ATV.

Minute 6594 FA Cup Pool

The Secretary reported that £3,119.80 had been paid out by the Football League in respect of FA Pool up to and including the Sixth Round. A sum of £500 had also been forwarded on by the League with regard to outstanding debt to the Club by Halifax Town.

Thursday 29th April 1971

Minute 6596 Manager's Report

Mr B. H. Clough, the Manager, reported on the probable teams for Saturday. Discussion took place regarding the Retain and Transfer list for the coming season

1971–72, and it was agreed that a full list of new contracts and wage increases in respect of all players would be available for the next meeting. Player, Roy Patrick would not be retained.

It was agreed that a donation of £25 be forwarded to Burton and District Football Association in respect of the Centenary Season commencing in August 1971.

Minute 6597 Share Capital Issue

The Secretary confirmed that no further information was at hand in respect of the proposed Share Capital Issue and the matter was still in the hands of Mr Timms. It was hoped that full progress reports and draft proposals for the Minute Book would be available at the next meeting.

Minute 6598 Balance at Bank

It was reported that the overdrawn balance at the bank on the Company's account to date stood at £82,000. To date, Season ticket sales for three days, 26th – 28th April, amounted to £22,000.

Minute 6600 Osmaston Stand Seats

A written quotation had now been received from Messrs Perks & Sons Limited of £11,250 for the proposed new seats under Osmaston Stand and this was confirmed. It was agreed that the prices of the new seats would fall in line with the present seat prices at the Osmaston End. £0.70 per game and £14.80 Season ticket with Cup Vouchers.

Minute 6601 Official Match Programme

Discussion took place regarding the Official Match Programme for 1971–72 season when proposals for a new Club newspaper type magazine were submitted by the Secretary.

After a lengthy discussion it was agreed that a meeting with the Programme editor on this matter would take place during the next couple of days and a final decision be reached before 3rd May.

Editor's Comments

Saturday 1st May 1971 was the last match for Dave Mackay against West Bromwich Albion. He was also named as Player of the Year, beating Roy McFarland and Kevin Hector. Mackay was pivotal in the promotion season from Division Two and his experience and guidance of the younger players in the first couple of seasons back in the First Division was invaluable. It is unfortunate that his talents were not seen in Europe due to the ban imposed by the football authorities.

Sam Longson wrote, 'His contribution to the revival of Derby County has been outstanding. Our admiration of him as a professional and as a man does not go far enough. Thanks a million.'

The 36-year-old Mackay said, 'My only regret at Derby was that after finishing fourth we were denied a place in Europe through no fault of the players.' In all he made 148 appearances, scoring 8 goals, and the current season was the first in his long career in which he played in every League game.

The Club was to embark on an 11-day end-of-season trip to Spain, staying in Calla Millor. They were to play two games, one a goalless draw against the island's premier team, Real Majorca in Palma, and was followed up by beating a local Select XI 4–0 with a goal from Dave Mackay, who turned out as a guest player after his departure from the club.

Monday 17th May 1971

Minute 6603 Manager's Report

The Assistant Manager, Mr P. Taylor came into the meeting and reported on the Club's Retain List. All the Playing Staff with the exception of Patrick had been retained and the Secretary outlined the various increases in salary that several players would receive next season.

Mr Taylor reported on the Club's successful tour of Majorca and the 0–0 draw with Real Majorca.

It was reported that a Derby County XI would play a Leicester City XI at Filbert Street on Tuesday 25th May 1971 in aid of the John Sjoberg Testimonial Fund.

Minute 6604 Share Capital Issue

The relevant documents and timetable in connection with the Issue had been passed on to the printers and Monday 7th June 1971 had been fixed as D-Day.

Minute 6605 Season tickets

The Secretary reported that Season ticket sales to date had reached £98,000, the first three weeks of sales.

Minute 6605a Balance at Bank

The overdrawn balance at the bank on the Club's account stood at £28,000 to date.

Minute 6606 New Osmaston Stand Seats

The Secretary outlined details of distribution in respect of regular supporters and the additional seats. Full details would be announced in the press in good time for the benefit of all supporters.

Minute 6607 New Magazine/Newspaper Style Programme

Details of the new style Club newspaper that would be sold through newsagents as well as at the ground was confirmed for 1971–72 season. A sum of £10,000 would be guaranteed for the season and it was agreed to accept the project for an initial one-year period.

Minute 6608 Clubroom and Licenced Bars

Discussion took place regarding the proposed charge and membership fee in respect of the new clubroom. It was agreed that the matter be discussed in detail at a later meeting. Application had been made for licenced bars to all parts of the ground for the next season. Bass Worthington (Midlands) Limited had agreed to donate £1,000 towards the bar equipment.

Minute 6609 Proposed New Stand

Confirmation that Derby Corporation were at present not considering a multi-use sports centre incorporating a football pitch was expressed in a letter from Mr Haines. It was confirmed that preparations of a scheme for the Normanton End would go ahead as agreed.

Thursday 27ᵗʰ May 1971

An apology for absence was received from Mr F. B. Walters who was at present in hospital.

The Chairman proposed that a letter be sent to Mrs Walters from the Directors.

The Chairman also welcomed Mr T. W. Rudd back to the Boardroom following his recent illness.

Minute 6611 Assistant Manager's Report

Mr P. Taylor reported that Terry Hennessey had come through the Club's friendly game with Leicester City without any further trouble and that he would be completely fit for the start of the new season.

Details in respect of the Club's pre-season tour of Germany were confirmed:

Wednesday 28ᵗʰ July 1971 v. Schalke FC at Gelsenkirchen

Friday 30ᵗʰ July 1971 v. SV Werder Bremen at Bremen

Sunday 1st August 1971 v. Maastricht (Holland) at Maastricht

Saturday 7th August 1971 v. Schalke FC at Derby Kick-off 7.30 p.m.

It was agreed to give wedding presents of Crown Derby to John Robson, Peter Daniel and Barry Butlin.

Minute 6612 Share Capital Issue

The Secretary confirmed that all documents had now been proofed and the Issue would be minuted at the next Meeting, with letters to Shareholders being posted out commencing 7th June 1971. Mr T. W. Rudd was elected as liaison Director for this operation.

Minute 6613 Season ticket Sales

The Secretary reported that Season ticket sales to date amounted to £170,000.

Minute 6615 "300" Clubroom

Discussion took place regarding the proposed membership fee for the new 300 Club. After discussion it was agreed that an average of £20 per member and £30 per man and wife with four prizes of £10 per month, an annual Car Draw and ties and scarves (Ladies) for all members.

It was agreed the Secretary make the necessary Press Statement.

Minute 6615 Balance at Bank

The Credit balance on the Club's Account to date stood at £36,000.

Minute 6616 Property, Shaftesbury Crescent

It was agreed the Club endeavour to purchase the properties No. 93, 95 and 97 Shaftesbury Crescent. It was agreed that Mr F. W. Innes would look into the matter on behalf of the Club.

Minute 6617 Texaco Cup

An invitation had been received from the Football League for the Club to take part in the 1971–72 Texaco Cup Competition. It was agreed that a decision be reached when the Manager returned from holiday.

Minute 6619 Official Club Badge and Copyright

It was agreed that the position of Copyright and a new Club image be looked into for the coming Season.

Minute 6620 Licenced Bars

A Progress Report on the Club's proposed Licenced Bars was submitted by the Secretary. The Fire and Police authorities had been satisfied with the proposed sites but the Police had queried the proposed opening hours. Stadia Catering would, however, be submitting relevant information to support our application and it was agreed to make further enquiries locally before finally submitting an application.

Monday 7ᵗʰ June 1971

Minute 6622 Manager's Report

The Chairman welcomed the Manager back from holiday and wished him well for the coming Season. Mr B. H. Clough reported that Norwich City had made an approach for Barry Butlin the fee in the region of £25,000 to £30,000.

Terry Hennessey was still receiving treatment at Etwall Rehabilitation Centre and it was hoped that this summer treatment would enable Hennessey to report back for pre-season training completely fit.

Minute 6623 Balance at Bank

It was reported that the Credit Balance on the Club's Account to date stood at £45,000.

Minute 6624 Property, 97 Shaftesbury Crescent

Mr F.W. Innes reported that the purchase of 97, Shaftesbury Crescent had been completed for £425.

Minute 6624 Season tickets 1971–72

The Secretary, reported that Season ticket sales to date had reached £182,000.

Minute 6625 Proposed 300 Club and Licenced Bars

It was reported that the Chairman would meet Chief Superintendent Shelley with a view to seeking the Police reaction to our proposals. It was agreed that should no objections be met an application for a 3.00 p.m. closing time be submitted.

Minute 6626 Staff Salaries

The Secretary outlined proposed salary increases for members of the administration. It was agreed that the matter be left to the Chairman and Secretary to finalise.

Minute 6627 Share Capital Issue

It was agreed the Secretary inform the Press of the proposed new Issue.

At this point Mr Farrow, Acting Club Solicitor joined.

Minute 6628 Rights Issue

In connection with the decision that additional permanent capital should be raised by a rights issue of the unissued shares of the Company, the following documents were produced to the Meeting and identified:

1. Print of a Circular Letter dated 7th June 1971 addressed to shareholders ('the Circular').
2. Print of a Provisional Allotment Letter dated 7th June 1971 in respect of the proposed Rights Issue.
3. Proposed Underwriting Agreement between the Company of the one part and Alan Farris of 62 Blagreaves Lane, Littleover, Derby a Director of Harris Tyre Co. Ltd, Cyril Frost of 'Purgate', Manchester Road, Tunstead, Melton, Chapel-en-le-Frith, Headmaster of Warmbrook Junior School.Arthur Clayton Pinder of Park Road, Chapel-en-le-Frith, Managing Director of T. Shelpley & Co. Ltd, Painters and Decorators, and Horace Frederick Porter of 1 Bramble Street, Derby a Director of F. Porter & Sons Limited, Corn & Seed Merchants, ('the Underwriters') of the other part.
4. Valuation of the freehold properties of the Company prepared by Messrs

Gerald Maynard & Co. dated 22ⁿᵈ April 1971.

5. Letter dated 22ⁿᵈ April 1971 from Mr B. E. Mason, F & A containing a statement of the net tangible assets of the Company based on the latest audited Balance Sheet of the Company dated 31ˢᵗ July 1970 prepared by Mr W. E. Mason, FCA and confirming the figures for the profits and losses of the Company as at the date of the latest audited Balance Sheet of the Company appearing in the Circular.

6. Statement from The National Westminster Bank Limited giving the amount of the Company's credit position as at 28ᵗʰ May 1971.

7. Statement of the bank balances and overdraft facilities.

The above documents were considered by the Board.

The meeting was informed that it was proposed to enter into an Agreement with the Underwriters and it was noted that the Agreement which was dated 28ᵗʰ May 1971 and signed by the Underwriters contained the terms to the effect that the Underwriters would subscribe such of the shares in respect of which provisional allotment is not accepted by shareholders at the price of £2 per share and would subscribe for fractional entitlements at the same price. The Agreement having been considered by the Board, IT WAS RESOLVED that the same be approved and passed under the seal of the Company and exchanged with the Underwriters.

IT WAS REPORTED that the Circular had been read and considered by each of the Directors in conjunction with the other documents mentioned above.

IT WAS CONFIRMED that all statements concerning the Company (and in particular the figures for net assets and profits and losses and the statement relating to current business) were accurate and there were no facts, the omission of which would make any statement misleading and it was also confirmed that nothing had occurred since the date of the latest audited accounts which had materially and adversely affected the financial position of the Company.

IT WAS ACCORDINGLY RESOLVED:

1. That the Directors collectively and individually accept full responsibility for the accuracy of the statements and information contained in the Circular and the Provisional Allotment Letter.

2. That the Circular and the Provisional Allotment Letter be approved and the Chairman be authorised to sign the Circular and the Secretary be authorised to sign the Provisional Allotment Letter.

3. That 13,852 shares of £1 each in the Company be provisionally allocated to those persons who were registered at the close of business on the 4th day of June, 1971 as holders of the issued shares of the Company rateably in accordance with their respective holdings at the price of £2 per share payable in full on acceptance on or before 28th June 1971, fractions of a share being disregarded.

4. That 1,494 shares being the number of shares representing entitlements be allotted to the Underwriters under the terms of the Underwriting Agreement.

5. That a print of the Circular and of the Provisional Allotment Letter having attached thereto the documents mentioned thereof be delivered to the Registrar of Companies for registration having been signed by or on behalf of all the Directors of the Company and subject thereto that prints thereof be despatched to shareholders of the Company on 7th June 1971.

6. That the estimate of expenses be approved:

Printers	£100
Mr W. E. Mason	£110
Messrs Gerald Maynard & Co.	£50
Counsel's Fees	£146.70
Solicitor's fees and Disbursements	£500

7. IT WAS FURTHER RESOLVED that pursuant to Article 67 of the Company's Articles of Association Mr S. Longson and Mr T. W. Rudd, Directors of the Company, be appointed a Committee of the Board:

a) To confirm in due course the provisional allotments in respect of those shareholders who accept.

b) To carry into effect the Underwriting Agreement.

c) To execute such other documents and to do such other things as may be necessary or desirable in connection with the issue.

It was agreed that pursuant to Mr F. B. Walters' letter of authority, Mr T. W.

Rudd would sign the Provisional Allotment Letter and the Letter to Shareholders on behalf of Mr F. B. Walters.

Thursday 17th June 1971

Minute 6631 Share Capital Issue

The Secretary reported that to date 110 shares had been claimed and a total of £220 had been received. The offer had a further 11 days to run. It was confirmed that on 28th June 1971 any outstanding balance of shares not claimed would be passed over to the Underwriters.

Minute 6632 Season tickets 1971–72

The Secretary outlined progress of Season ticket sales and reported that £221,000 had already been sold. It was estimated that a further £20,000 of sales could be expected before the commencement of the season.

Minute 6633 Balance at Bank

The Credit Ledger of the Company's account stood at £57,000 of which £30,000 had been put on deposit.

Outstanding accounts for the past months had been passed by the Finance Committee and charges to the value of £13,404 were agreed to be paid.

Minute 6636 Texaco Cup

It was confirmed that the Club had accepted the Football League's invitation to compete in the 1971–72 Texaco Cup Competition.

	HOME			AWAY	

League Division 1

22/08/1970	Stoke City	2–0	15/08/1970	Chelsea	1–2
26/08/1970	Ipswich Town	2–0	19/08/1970	Wolverhampton Wanderers	4–2
02/09/1970	Coventry City	3–4	29/08/1970	Huddersfield Town	0–0
05/09/1970	Newcastle United	1–2	12/09/1970	Southampton	0–4
19/09/1970	Burnley	1–0	26/09/1970	West Bromwich Albion	1–2
03/10/1970	Tottenham Hotspur	1–1	10/10/1970	Everton	1–1
17/10/1970	Chelsea	1–2	31/10/1970	Arsenal	0–2
24/10/1970	Leeds United	0–2	14/11/1970	Manchester City	1–1
07/11/1970	Liverpool	0–0	28/11/1970	Nottingham Forest	4–2
21/11/1970	Blackpool	2–0	12/12/1970	Crystal Palace	0–0
05/12/1970	West Ham United	2–4	19/12/1970	Stoke City	0–1
26/12/1970	Manchester United	4–4	16/01/1971	Ipswich Town	1–0
09/01/1971	Wolverhampton Wanderers	2–1	06/02/1971	West Ham United	4–1
17/02/1971	Crystal Palace	1–0	20/02/1971	Blackpool	1–0
27/02/1971	Arsenal	2–0	06/03/1971	Leeds United	0–1
13/03/1971	Manchester City	0–0	20/03/1971	Liverpool	0–2
31/03/1971	Nottingham Forest	1–2	27/03/1971	Newcastle United	1–3
03/04/1971	Huddersfield Town	3–2	07/04/1971	Tottenham Hotspur	1–2
12/04/1971	Southampton	0–0	10/04/1971	Manchester United	2–1
17/04/1971	Everton	3–1	24/04/1971	Burnley	2–1
01/05/1971	West Bromwich Albion	2–0	27/04/1971	Coventry City	0–0

League Cup

| 08/09/1970 | Halifax Town | 3–1 | 27/10/1970 | Coventry City | 0–1 |
| 07/10/1970 | Millwall | 4–2 | | | |

FA Cup

| 23/01/1971 | Wolverhampton Wanderers | 2–1 | 02/01/1971 | Chester City | 2–1 |
| | | | 13/02/1971 | Everton | 0–1 |

Watney Cup

05/08/1970	Sheffield United	1–0	01/08/1970	Fulham	5–3
08/08/1970	Manchester United	4–1			

Postponed Game

30/01/1971	Nottingham Forest

Friendlies

14/12/1970	British Olympic XI	0–1	05/05/1971	Real Majorca	0–0
			13/05/1971	Calla Millor XI	4–0

Testimonials

24/03/1971	Coventry City (Webster)	2–1	12/10/1970	Peterborough United	1–2
			25/05/1971	Leicester City	0–1

SEASON SUMMARY

Football League Division One:	9th
FA Cup:	Fifth Round
Football League Cup:	Fifth Round
Watney Cup:	Winners
Central League:	Runners-Up
Average League Attendance:	31,367
Highest Attendance:	40,567 v. Wolverhampton Wanderers
Top League Scorers:	John O'Hare (13)
	Kevin Hector (11)
	Alan Hinton (10)

SEASON 1971–72

1971–72 brought about many changes off the field of play, all of which were noticeable and long-lasting in many ways. The first of these was a redesign of the Club badge, moving away from the familiar ram's head to a more modern design of a full-bodied ram. Headed-up by Secretary Webb and Director Michael Keeling, they went to Product Support (Graphics) on Slack Lane, Derby in order to have a new logo designed. Tony Hoyle (a Leeds United fan) was the artist responsible and after more than 40 different sketches, they settled on one design in particular that is still in use today.

The second change was in the Club's colours. The traditional white shirts and black shorts that had been in use for the majority of the Club's history to date were to be changed to white shirt with blue shorts, making them look very similar to the England kit, hoping for a similar change in mentality to that experienced when Leeds United changed their club colours to all white to mimic Real Madrid.

There had been many changes completed around the stadium over the course of the summer to improve the facilities, which was the main reason for Derby not participating in the Anglo-Italian Cup tournament during the late summer. Some 1,500 new seats had been installed in the middle tier of the Osmaston Stand, which reduced the overall stadium capacity to 40,000, of which 14,000 were seats. The overall aim was to redesign the stadium to reach a 50,000 capacity and a new Normanton Stand had been discussed during the previous season.

The new Sportsman's Club (previously referred to as the 300 Club) was now complete and open for a fee of £20 per season, with a maximum of 250 guests. The room itself was split over two levels with pine panelling throughout and fully-fitted bar and cloakroom making it comparable with any other facility in the country. At its opening, Chairman Longson said, 'When we won promotion, we found ourselves with 20,000 extra supporters – and a ground below First Division standards. The Ley Stand was a huge step in the right direction and this club room is another step down the same path.'

As well as these changes, there were new turnstile entrances, additional drainage under the pitch, upgraded and new catering facilities around the ground and even a gable in the middle of the 'B' Stand roof had been added, in all costing around £60,000.

Roy McFarland was the appointed captain as successor to Dave Mackay – a difficult choice as there were several possible candidates: Terry Hennessey was now the captain of the Wales national team, Alan Durban had also captained Wales, and recent arrival Colin Todd was captain at Sunderland and also the England Under-23 team.

Derby had made an offer to West Bromwich Albion for the transfer of England centre-forward and Eastwood-born Jeff Astle, but was turned down and no further approach or improved offer was made.

Thursday 15th July 1971

Minute 6638 Manager's Report

The Manager, Mr B. H. Clough reported that Norwich City had made an offer of £30,000 in respect of Barry Butlin. It was agreed no action be taken at present until the position regarding Jeff Astle of West Bromwich Albion became clear.

Butlin was at present in hospital suffering from a cracked skull that he received during training.

It was confirmed that all clubs had been notified that Wignall, Green and Richardson were available for offers.

It was agreed that a donation of £100 be forwarded to Linton United FC in respect of Jeff Bourne.

Minute 6639 Share Capital Issue

The Secretary reported the following in respect of the Club's Share Issue:

Original Shares allotted prior to Issue   6,148
Taken up by Shareholders from Issue   6,427

Balance taken up by the Underwriters   7,425

                                         20,000

A total cash figure of £27,704 had been banked in connection with the Issue.

The following Shareholders had increased their holdings and Certificates had been completed and forwarded:

[selected]

	Shares	Amount Paid
K. Gregory, Quarndon	340	£680
H. Payne, Ripley	250	£500
Bass Worthington, Burton	2,000	£4,000
Archer/Robotham/Jeffrey, Rolleston	2,434	£4,868
R. Kirkland, Long Eaton	240	£480
K. Turner, Borrowash	476	£952
Underwriters	7,425	£14,850

Minute 6641 Balance at Bank

The credit balance on the Club's account to date stood at £59,000.

Minute 6642 Season tickets 1971–72

The Secretary reported that Season ticket sales had reached £222,000 to date.

Minute 6643 Manager & Assistant Manager's Salary & Incentives 1971–72

It was agreed that the Manager, Mr B. H. Clough would receive a salary of £10,000 per annum commencing 1st August 1971, £999.99 of which would be paid annually for him by the club in the form of an Insurance Policy.

Mr P. Taylor, Assistant Manager would remain at £5,000 per annum but would receive a bonus of £250 in respect of season 1970–71. The company would purchase a Rover 2000 for Mr Taylor's use.

Bonuses – Manager & Asst. Manager

Incentives agreed upon for 1971–72 season:

1st in Football League Division One   £5,000 each

2nd	£3,000 each
3rd, 4th, 5th, 6th	£2,000 each
7th, 8th	£1,000 each
9th-10th	£500 each

FA Cup

£5,000 each for reaching the Cup Final

£3,000	Semi-final
£1500	Sixth Round
£1000	Fifth Round
£500	Fourth Round

Football League Cup

£5,000 each for reaching Cup Final

£3,000 each	Semi-final
£1,500 each	Sixth Round
£1,000 each	Fifth Round
£500 each	Fourth Round

Europe

£1500 each if the Club qualifies for Europe

Minute 6644 Playing Staff Incentives 1971–72

Football League (Paid during the season):

When the team is in the 1st or 2nd position £50 per week

When the team is in the 3rd or 4th position £45 per week

When the team is in the 5th or 6th position £40 per week

When the team is in the 7th or 8th position £35 per week

When the team is in the 9th to 11th position inclusive £25 per week

When the team is in the 12th position £20 per week

When the team is in the 13th position £15 per week

When the team is in the 14th position £10 per week

When the team is in the 15th position £5 per week

Football League (Paid at the end of the season) pro rata according to the number of appearances made:

1st position in Football League £2500

2nd position in Football League £2000

3rd position in Football League £1500

4th position in Football League £1000

5th position in Football League £500

FA Cup		Football League Cup	
Round 3	£20	Round 2	£10
4	£50	3	£30
5	£70	4	£50
6	£100	5	£100
Semi-final	£250	Semi-final	£150 each leg
Final	£500	Final	£500

An additional £500 to be paid if qualifying for a European competition during the period of contract, together with £200 per round after the first round has been played.

The aforementioned bonuses outlined will be paid to the 11 players taking part in League matches, plus the substitute. Three additional players named weekly as making up the pool of 15 players will be paid one third of the aforementioned bonus.

Texaco Cup

First Round: £10 per appearance in each leg

£20 per player if team qualifies for Second Round

Second Round: £20 per appearance in each leg

£40 per player if team qualifies for Semi-final

Semi-final: £25 per appearance in each leg

£50 per player if team qualifies for Final

Cup Final: £30 per appearance in each leg

£100 per player if team wins Final

Minute 6645 Central League

Permission has been received from the Central League to present medals to the value of £10 each for players making more than 14 appearances in last year's successful team.

Monday 9ᵗʰ August 1971

Minute 6647 Manager's Report

Mr P. Taylor, Assistant Manager was called into the Meeting to report on relevant team matters since the last meeting.

John Richardson had been transferred to Notts County for a fee of £8,880, breakdown as follows:

5% to Football League per Rule	£440
5% to Richardson as per Rule	£440
Net Fee to Derby County	£8000
	£8880

Roy McFarland had returned to Derby and should be in a position to commence training following a final examination by the Specialist on Monday next.

Les Green had been fined and suspended for a two-week period in respect of non-attendance for training whilst the first team party was away on tour in Germany.

Minute 6648 Pre-Season Tour 1971–72

The Chairman reported on a very successful tour of Germany and Holland, the team winning all the games and of the wonderful spirit throughout the whole party.

Results:

28th July 1971	Schalke 04 1	Derby County 3
30th July 1971	Werder Bremen 1	Derby County 2
3rd August 1971	Go Ahead Deventer 0	Derby County 2

The Secretary reported a financial profit of £1,400 on the tour with an approximate Net Profit of £2,000 from the home game v. Schalke 04.

Minute 6649 Season tickets – Season 1971–72

The Secretary reported that Season ticket sales to date had reached the sum of £234,000.

Minute 6650 Television

It was reported that the following games would be televised from the Baseball Ground:

Company	Date	Opponents
ATV	14/8/71	Manchester United
BBC	28/8/71	Southampton

Minute 6651 Balance at Bank

The Company's credit finance at the Bank to date stood at £53,000. The final payment on Colin Todd of £38,000 was due and would be paid to Sunderland forthwith.

Minute 6653 Proposed New Normanton Stand

A letter from Mosby, Haines Partnership was read confirming that they had made formal planning application to the local authority in respect of the proposed new stand. It was agreed that no further action be taken until the reaction of the local authority was voiced.

Editor's Comments

John Richardson had been a first-choice defender since the 1965–66 season and survived one season under Brian Clough before losing his place to the likes of Ron Webster and John Robson. He had played just 14 games in the last three seasons and was now thought to be wanting regular first team football.

Ernie Hutchinson and Roger Patrick, both forwards, had also left the club to join Ballymena (Dublin) and Ilkeston Town respectively.

Roy McFarland had been troubled by a bout of flu and completely missed the pre-season tour and so his fitness had suffered, having done only one week of the hard pre-season training. He was some way behind the rest of the squad and would be missing from first team action until fully recovered and fit.

Archie Gemmill's son Scot had been taken into hospital whilst he was away on the tour, with a relaxed muscle problem in his neck that had to be operated upon within a distinct timeframe, being so young. Fortunately, all was well with him but he would require further manipulation and physiotherapy to finally rectify the problem, and was an obvious distraction for the player.

Another new innovation for the coming season was the introduction of a newspaper to replace the traditional match programme. The newspaper was the first of its kind in English football and a sample version was issued for the previous week's firendly match against Schalke and was given away at the game. Derby won the fixture 2–0 in front of 13,051 generating receipts of £5,739.20.

The first real issue of *The Ram* (the title of the new publication) would be available in newsagents throught Derbyshire on the Friday morning prior to the Saturday fixture, and would usually have 12 tabloid-sized pages, with at least the front and back being in colour. For midweek matches on a Wednesday the paper would be available for delivery with your usual daily paper.

The first League fixture of the season was against Manchester United and Roy McFarland was still unable to take his place in the team, which meant Terry Hennessey would play at centre-half and also assume the captain's role. Hennessey had now fully recovered from the two cartilage operations from the previous season and played in all the pre-season games.

The Ram newspaper had been well received and sales via the newsagent network had seen over 45,000 copies sold for the first game, more than double the previous season average sales figure, and more than actually attended the game.

The large attendances of the last couple of seasons had brought major traffic issues in and around the area that were compounded by the stadium's location in amongst the narrow streets and terraced houses. The parking restrictions were being extended, and where possible supporters were advised to begin to use the Park 'n' Ride services that ran from Mickleover, Allestree, Chaddesden, Ascot Drive and Normanton Barracks. These services would bring the fans direct to the ground and park along Reeves Road adjacent to the ground.

As an added incentive to get more fans travelling this way, services would be started from other areas if there was a minimum of 60 supporters. The football club were willing to underwrite the cost of these services to get them started.

Wednesday 18th August 1971

Minute 6655 Manager's Report
Mr B. H. Clough reported on relevant team matters during the past week and that Barry Butlin was now back in training, along with Roy McFarland.

Les Green had been released on a free transfer to South African club Durban City. A cheque for £750 to cover Green's debts with the Club was to be paid by Durban City.

Minute 6657 Balance at Bank

The credit balance on the Company's account stood to date at £44,000. Payments being due to Dyson & Co. (£12,000) and Perks & Co. (£10,000) within the next week.

Minute 6658 Insurance

The Secretary outlined increases in general ground and fire insurance for 1971–72. An additional premium would have to be paid in respect of Public Liability following the Ibrox Disaster.

Minute 6659 Season tickets 1971–72

Season ticket sales to date stood at £239,000 for season 1971–72.

Minute 6660 Share Transfers

The following share transfers were presented and passed. Certificates being signed by S. Longson (Chairman) and Sir Robertson King, KBE.

The Underwriters to

Mr F. B. Walters 500 shares

Mr M. Keeling	1,200 shares
Mr F. W. Innes	1,200 shares
Mr T. W. Rudd	1,200 shares
Mr S. C. Bradley	800 shares
Mr S. Longson	700 shares

Editor's Comments

Les Green was signed for £8,000 from Rochdale in 1968 and became an ever-present member of the Division Two championship team. He made

129 appearances and his last game for the Club was the 4–4 Boxing Day home draw against Manchester United.

In Green's place, 16-year-old John Turner stepped into the Reserve team and made a good impression in his first game against Manchester United, which was played at Macclesfield as Old Trafford had been closed due to continuing crowd trouble.

The Ibrox Disaster, home of Rangers FC happened on 2nd January 1971 in a match against rivals Celtic. A crush amongst the crowd at an exit stairway saw 66 fans die and another 200 injured, the worst stadium disaster until that point. The Rangers club were taken to court by the families of the dead fans and all clubs were having their Public Liability premiums increased as a result.

Thursday 26th August 1971

Minute 6662 Manager's Report

The Manager, Mr B. H. Clough informed the meeting that the Club had no injury problems at the moment and of the probable team to meet Southampton at the Baseball Ground next Saturday.

Arrangements for the visit to Dundee in the Texaco Cup were confirmed. The team would stay up North for the remainder of the week in preparation for the League game v. Newcastle United at St James' Park.

It was confirmed that the Manager would be allowed to claim 10p per mile petrol allowance in respect of mileage completed on Club business. The figure being the current allowance obtained from the Automobile Association.

It was agreed that P. Taylor be informed in writing from the Secretary that the new Club car placed at his disposal must be driven only by himself except of course in extreme circumstances.

Minute 6663 Sportsmen's Club

It was agreed that in view of the limited number of memberships received for the current year membership cards would admit two persons. Arrangements to install a Colour TV Set would also be completed within the next few weeks.

Minute 6664 Slaughter & May

The Secretary confirmed that a final payment of £199 had been paid to Slaughter & May making a total settlement figure of £593.77 out of the original account of £764.78.

Minute 6665 Property – Holcombe Street

It was agreed that the Club were not interested at the present time in purchasing the Holcombe Street works of S. Robinson & Co.

Minute 6666 Season tickets 1971–72

The Secretary confirmed that an almost final figure of £241,000 had been banked in respect of Season tickets for 1971–72.

Minute 6669 Osmaston Stand Re-Sheeting

An estimate of £3,640 in respect of re-sheeting the Osmaston Stand was confirmed. The work by Dysons & Co. would commence following the Leeds United Football League Cup tie and take approximately 14 days to complete.

Editor's Comments

Although Season ticket sales were documented in terms of financial value, currently stated as £241,000, this equated to approximately 18,000 tickets, a new club record.

Thursday 9ᵗʰ September 1971

Minute 6671 Manager's Report

The Manager, Mr B. H. Clough reported on the relevant team matters of the past week.

It was reported that the Football League had arranged the Second Round Football League Cup replay with Leeds United for Monday 27ᵗʰ September 1971.

An offer of £15,000 for Jim McDonagh, goalkeeper of Rotherham United had been rejected by the Yorkshire Club.

It was agreed that a Club photograph would be taken at 9.45 a.m. on Thursday 23ʳᵈ September 1971.

Minute 6672 Balance at Bank

The Company's position to date at the Bank was as follows:

Deposit Account £30,780; Current overdrawn £29,000.

It was agreed that the £30,000 be taken from Deposit. It was also agreed that an early meeting with the Bank Manager be arranged.

Minute 6673 BBC Television

The Secretary reported that the following games at the Baseball Ground would be covered by BBC TV:

Saturday 9th October 1971 v. Tottenham Hotspur

Saturday 23rd October 1971 v. Arsenal

Editor's Comments

The 36,023 fans that attended the League Cup tie with Leeds United on 8ᵗʰ September generated record receipts for the club of £18,360.30 despite the game being not all-ticket (indeed, Leeds had returned a significant portion of their seat allocation for the game) and was the first time that the new Cup Voucher scheme had been used. Apart from three seats in the Ley Stand having duplicate tickets issued, the system worked perfectly and justified its introduction.

The new receipts record beat the previous one set in the Wolverhampton Wanderers FA Cup tie last season in front of a 40,000 crowd, despite terracing prices remaining the same. The reason for the increase was a slight increase in seat prices and the Osmaston Lower Tier was now all seated.

The Texaco Cup competition kicked off on 15th September, this being the second season of the competition, and 16 clubs (6 from England, 6 from Scotland and 4 from Ireland) were invited to enter. The automatic qualifiers for the main European competitions were Arsenal, Leeds United, Tottenham Hotspur, Wolverhampton Wanderers, Liverpool and Chelsea and so were not invited. With the League Cup competition now compulsory, Manchester United and Everton declined the invitation leaving Derby, Stoke City, Coventry City, Manchester City and Huddersfield Town (who finished ahead of Nottingham Forest on goal average in the First Division table) as the competing teams.

The format of the competition was a perfect opportunity for the club to organise trips, for the management to try out new styles of play and also to get to grips with the psychology of the two-legged matches, as used in the main European competitions.

Derek Dougan, who helped Wolverhampton Wanderers win the first Texaco Cup competition, agreed that the Texaco competition was a perfect introduction to 'the experience of the home and away tactics of Europe, and it was a first-class rehearsal'.

Derby were already working closely with Texaco with large parts of the stands having Texaco boards adorning them, in what was the most lucrative deal of its kind ever negotiated by a League club.

The first round was to pair the English and Scottish teams together and the four Irish teams would play each other. Derby were drawn against Dundee United.

Friday 24th September 1971

An apology was received from Sir Robertson King, KBE who was indisposed.

Minute 6676 Manager's Report

Mr B. H. Clough reported on relevant team matters and that Terry Hennessey would not be fit for selection this coming weekend due to a bout of flu.

Barry Butlin had refused a possible transfer to Norwich City for a Net Fee of £28,500 on the grounds of his wife not wanting to leave Derby.

The signing of Roger Davies from Worcester City for a fee of £14,000 was confirmed. The player would receive £250 signing bonus as per Football League Rule which would be spread over the period of his contract.

The date of the friendly game v. Swindon Town was confirmed for Tuesday 12th October 1971, kick-off 7.30 p.m.

It was confirmed that the Club would employ a full-time electrician in respect of ground maintenance.

Minute 6678 Balance at Bank

The overdrawn balance on the Club's account to date stood at £5,000. A donation of £5,000 having been received from Derby County Promotions and Worcester City had been paid their £14,000.

Minute 6680 Football League – Extraordinary General Meeting

It was reported that an Extraordinary General Meeting of The Football League Limited had been called for 14th October 1971 in respect of

a. Rule 40a.

b. Discipline on the field of play.

The Chairman and Secretary would also attend a meeting of Midland Clubs at Wolverhampton prior to the Football League Meeting.

Editor's Comments

Three Derby County players were selected by Sir Alf Ramsey in the Football League side that played the League of Ireland in Dublin on Wednesday evening – Roy McFarland, Colin Todd and Kevin Hector, although Todd did not start but came on for the last 30 minutes.

The Sun newspaper headlined the signing of Roger Davies as 'Clough beats them all in race for the Golden Boy' amidst rumours of a dozen clubs, including Arsenal, chasing his signature. Clough said, 'This was a case of while others watched, waited and wondered about it, we acted.' Davies took his place in the Reserve team to play West Bromwich Albion on the previous Saturday (18th March) and scored a last-minute winner despite feeling the pace of the game during the latter stages.

The Football League Rule 40a, as we have seen detailed in the documented player transfers, relates to the 10% levy on all transfers, with 5% automatically going to the Football League and the other 5% to the player. The member clubs were unhappy that the 5% going to the Football League applied to free transfers and also there was a minimum of £500 to pay; the clubs were not arguing against the levy, but which transfers it applied to. With Third and Fourth Division clubs financially struggling already, it seemed unfair to charge them £500 should they wish to sign a free transfer player, and would certainly make them stop and think about it and was unhelpful to all concerned. The same amount also applied to a youngster joining his first club.

Monday 11ᵗʰ October 1971

Minute 6682 Manager's Report

Mr B. H. Clough, the Manager reported that G. Pycroft who was employed as a Scout with the Company would have his employment terminated.

Details of the transfer of Graham Moseley from Blackburn Rovers were confirmed as follows:

£944	5% to Player as per Rule
£944	5% to Football League as per Rule 40a
<u>£17,000</u>	<u>Blackburn Rovers</u>
£18,888	

It was confirmed that Ron Webster and Jim Walker would both be doubtful for selection this coming weekend due to injury.

The following extra games were confirmed:

Tuesday 26th October 1971 v. Swindon Town (away) Friendly

Monday 15th November 1971 v. Werder Bremen (home) Friendly

Central League – rearranged dates:

Friday 15th October 1971 v. Sheffield Wednesday Reserves 7.30 p.m.

Friday 29th October 1971 v. Nottingham Forest Reserves 7.30 p.m.

Minute 6683 Derby Schoolboys

It was reported that following their two games at the Baseball Ground v. Birmingham & Sheffield Boys, The Association had received a cash figure of £90. This together with advance ticket sales reached a total of £160.

Minute 6684 Football League – Extraordinary General Meeting

The Secretary reported on the Meeting of Midland Club Chairmen and Secretaries that was held in Wolverhampton on Thursday 7th October 1971 with reference to Rule 40a and the Football League's forthcoming Meeting at Lytham on 14th October 1971.

It was agreed that Derby County in line with other Midland Clubs opposed any change in the present Rule 40a that disposed of the present 5% signing on levy.

Minute 6685 Draft Accounts For Year Ending 31st July 1971

The Draft Accounts to 31st July 1971 were presented to the Meeting and discussion took place regarding several items included therein. The main feature being a profit for the year of £624 after paying out a net figure on transfers of £170,000 together with approximately £40,000 on general ground improvements. Donations from Derby County Promotions amounted to £75,000.

The Annual General Meeting was arranged for Friday 19th November 1971 to be held in the new Clubroom at the Baseball Ground commencing at 10.30 a.m. Directors retiring by Rotation from Office being F. B. Walters, Esq., and T. W. Rudd, Esq.

Minute 6686 Balance at Bank

The overdrawn balance on the Club's account to date stood at £19,000. A further donation of £5,000 from Derby County Promotions having been received.

Minute 6688 Electronic Scoreboard

It was reported that the possibilities of obtaining an Electronic Scoreboard for the Ground were being looked into at present. Costs ranged from £12,000 to £17,000 for the various schemes and systems.

Editor's Comments

Derby made five changes for the Dundee United match from the team that lost against Leeds United in a League Cup replay just two days earlier with Peter Daniel, Tony Bailey, Barry Butlin, Jim Walker and Terry Hennessey all coming into the team replacing Webster, McFarland, Todd, O'Hare and Hector. Terry Hennessey was a late replacement as he had been suffering from flu and was only flown up in the plane carrying the supporters in mid-afternoon. These changes were also with a view to the difficult game at Newcastle United at the weekend coming up. On the morning of the game, Brian Clough told the local Dundee newspapers, 'we have a load of injuries, but we have come here to win. We don't like losing at Derby.'

There had been some suggestion from various parties that Derby deliberately fielded an under-strength team (the missing players all had medical certificates) for the game, having made five changes. Manchester City had already been found guilty of that offence and their £1,000 participation fee in the competition was withheld. Derby's view was that to do this would have been an insult to the other competing clubs, supporters and not least the sponsor of the tournament who also was the Club's own stadium sign sponsor.

For the weekend trip to Newcastle (which Derby won 1–0), the five players who sat out the Dundee game all came back into the team with Gemmill being replaced by Durban.

It was announced that Derby County was to stage the Under-23 international match between England and Scotland on February 16th 1972. This was seen as a huge achievement given that 18 months previously the club was heavily fined and severely reprimanded for administrative failings, and to be selected has the upmost approval of the highest of the Football Association and the public would support the match in large numbers.

UEFA had increased their minimum standard for floodlighting, which was far in advance of those imposed by the Football League. This meant that any club wishing to play in the major European club competitions had to adopt these new standards. The driving force behind this was colour television, where pitch illumination had to be twice as bright as that used for black and white coverage. Plans were already being discussed to add new floodlighting as part of a wider stadium refit, but qualification for European competition would bring that forward quickly.

There was plenty of international recognition for the squad during the week with Terry Hennessey and Alan Durban playing for Wales against Finland, where Durban was on the scoresheet with a long-range shot. Meanwhile, both of Scotland's goals in their 2–1 over Portugal came from the Derby camp with O'Hare and Gemmill netting, Gemmill coming back into the side with new Manager Tommy Docherty following a rather disastrous debut in Belgium. Roy McFarland was one of the better players for England as they struggled to 3–2 in Switzerland.

Prior to the Tottenham Hotspur game, Clough commented that he wanted the attendances to grow by an extra 6,000–8,000. He went on to say, 'With an extra two players we would certainly do it [win the League title]. To get the money to buy those players we want gates of 40,000.'

It was also announced that West German team Werder Bremen would play an international floodlit friendly on Monday 15th November. Derby had played the same opponents during pre-season, winning 2–1, and a return game had been suggested at that time. The Germans commented that they had played 'one of the best English club sides we have seen here in ten years or more'. The best seat tickets to cost £1 and Popside terrace tickets were to be 30p.

During the previous two weeks, the whole of the Osmaston Stand had been recovered. The grey corrugated iron sheeting had been removed and replaced with more modern plastic-coated aluminium, with additional Perspex panels to allow more light into the stairways and seating areas.

Thursday 28th October 1971

Minute 6690 Manager's Report

The Manager reported that Ron Webster was now fully recovered from his injury and would be considered for team selection against Nottingham Forest.

Graham Moseley had received a cracked finger in the friendly against Swindon Town on 26th October 1971.

It was confirmed that the Youth Team would play Louth United on Tuesday 2nd November 1971 in the FA Youth Cup First Round.

Mr T. W. Rudd undertook to obtain the present address of Les Green who was understood to be back in England. A fee of £700 was still owing to the Club in respect of the player's transfer to Durban City.

A lengthy discussion took place regarding the condition of the playing pitch. It was agreed that it was in general poor condition for a First Division Club and a decision as to further action would be taken at a future meeting.

The Chairman, Mr S. Longson confirmed that the Management, Players and Staff would receive the usual Xmas Turkeys from the Board of Directors for Xmas 1971.

Minute 6691 Balance at Bank

The overdrawn Balance on the Club's Account to date stood at £8,000.

Minute 6692 Independent TV at the Baseball Ground

The Secretary confirmed that ATV would cover the home game v. Sheffield United on Saturday 20th November 1971.

Minute 6693 Football League – Extraordinary General Meeting

The Chairman reported on the recent Football League Extraordinary General Meeting when it was agreed that the proposition to amend Rule 40(A) in respect of abolishing the present 5% levy on transfer fees would not be altered. Negotiations would, however, continue to remove the present minimum £500 signing bonus in respect of Professional Players signing on Free Transfers.

Minute 6695 Proposed New Stand

The Chairman reported on a meeting with Mr Haines of Mosby, Haines and Co. in respect of the proposed new Normanton Stand. Planning application would be submitted and at present it was felt that Derby Corporation had no objections to the Club's proposals. A decision as to the actual go ahead once planning permission had been granted would be discussed at a future date.

The good wishes of the Board of Directors were extended to Mr S. Longson for his forthcoming holiday (in Torremolinos) through Mr F. W. Innes.

Editor's Comments

The Swindon Town friendly on 28th October was an event to mark the opening of the new £300,000 main stand, and the Swindon team featured Dave Mackay. 6,236 fans attended to see the 1–1 draw, with Frank Wignall scoring a late equalising goal. Graham Moseley was a second-half substitute, but broke the fourth finger of his right hand during his appearance which would keep him out of action for the Reserves and England Youth teams.

The international friendly against Werder Bremen on November 8th gave the club an opportunity to produce a programme for the Saturday match at Wolverhampton Wanderers, and an issue was distributed in the usual way on the Friday morning. This issue was to also cover the Monday evening fixture.

Roy McFarland had been injured against Nottingham Forest and the back injury sustained was to keep him out of the matches at Stoke City in the Texaco Cup and the home game against Crystal Palace, after failing a fitness test. This also meant that he was withdrawn from the England squad that was to play Switzerland at Wembley Stadium four days later, on 10th November, in which Larry Lloyd of Liverpool was to take his place.

Archie Gemmill withdrew from the Scotland squad due to an attack of shingles, leaving John O'Hare as the sole Derby representative on duty in the latest round of international matches. He was the goal scorer in the 1–0 win over Belgium. O'Hare had now scored all but one of Scotland's goals in their last eight games, prompting Scotland Manager Tommy Docherty to describe him as 'one of the best target men in the world'.

November 11th: Frank Wignall was in talks with Mansfield Town over proposed move.

Terry Hennessey and Alan Durban had both been withdrawn from the Wales squad to play away in Romania on 24th November as that clashed with the semi-final, first leg, of the Texaco Cup competition against Newcastle United. Brian Clough was particularly upset with the Welsh Football administrators for not checking domestic fixtures before arranging international matches, although in fairness to Welsh FA, it was a European Championship qualification match and they probably did not have too much say in the date on which it could be played.

Thursday 18ᵗʰ November 1971

Minute 6697 Manager's Report

Mr B. H. Clough, the Manager, reported that confirmation had been received from the FA that Todd and Robson would be released from the Under-23s party for the Texaco Cup Semi-Final at Derby on Wednesday 24ᵗʰ November 1971.

Details of Frank Wignall's transfer to Mansfield Town were confirmed as follows:

£6,000 Gross Fee

£300 - 5% to Football League

£300 - 5% to Player

£5,400 Net Fee to Derby County

Deferred payments being agreed, £2,000 within seven days and the balance of the fee by April 1972.

It was agreed that the team would spend three to four days in Greece playing one match whilst out there on 15ᵗʰ December 1971. A match guarantee of £4,000 plus expenses for a party of 21 had been offered. It was confirmed that the official party would consist of 14 players, Assistant Manager, Mr P. Taylor, Coach, J. Gordon and four Directors. Messrs. S. Longson, T. W. Rudd, F. W. Innes, and M. Keeling. The London-based journalist who had arranged the trip would make up the party of 21.

The Manager reported that the following junior players had been dealt with for breach of Club Disciplinary Rules:

A. Lewis £10 fine plus 1 week's suspension

P. Phelan £10 fine plus 1 week's suspension

T. Thompson £5 fine

J. Turner £5 fine

C. Griffin £5 fine

The Secretary confirmed that the Football League and Football Association had been notified accordingly.

Minute 6698 Balance at Bank
The Club's overdrawn balance at the Bank to date stood at £10,500.

Minute 6699 Annual General Meeting
The Secretary outlined details and procedure for the AGM which would take place on Friday 19th November 1971 at 10.30 a.m. No nominations having been received from Shareholders in respect of the Retiring Directors.

Minute 6701 TV at the Baseball Ground
Confirmation of the following games that would be televised:

Wednesday 25th November 1971 Texaco Cup Semi-Final ITV v. Newcastle United

Saturday 4th December 1971 Football League BBC v. Manchester City

Minute 6702 Secretary
The Chairman reported that a Company Car had been purchased for the Secretary's use. The car being a Ford Cortina 1600, valued at £1,355.

Share Transfer
S. Longson to:

B. H. Clough,

Ferrers Way

Darley Abbey   50 shares   No 13976 to 14025

Editor's Comments

According to *Sam's Story*, Longson's autobiography (p. 82), he says, 'I gave him some Derby County shares. I knew as far as football law was concerned, that it was wrong, but I felt I wasn't giving them to him not as our club manager, but as a friend.'

Friday 19th November 1971

Annual General Meeting

PRESENT: Mr S. Longson (Chairman)

                  Mr F. B. Walters

                  Mr S. C. Bradley

                  Mr T. W. Rudd

                  Mr F. W. Innes

                  Mr M. Keeling

An apology was received from Sir Robertson King, KBE absent from the Meeting.
31 Shareholders attended.

IN ATTENDANCE: Mr A. S. Webb – Secretary

                        Mr W. E. Mason – Auditor

Notice Convening the Meeting

The Secretary read the notice convening the Meeting.

Minutes of the Last Ordinary General Meeting

The Minutes of the last Ordinary General Meeting held on Friday 4th December 1970 were read, approved and signed.

Auditor's Report

The representative of the Auditors read the report of the Auditors to the Meeting.

Confirmation was received that the change of name of Auditor from W. E. Mason Esq., (Individual) to the firm, H. R. Horne & Partners (Chartered Accountants) was agreed.

Directors' Report & Accounts

The Chairman proposed:

'That the Directors' Report , the Revenue Account for the year ended 31st July 1971, and the Balance Sheet at that date, be and hereby be approved and adopted'.

Mr L. Overton seconded the proposition, and after dealing with general questions on accounts, the Chairman put the resolution to the Meeting, and declared it carried.

Election of Directors

Special notice having been given to the Company, in accordance with the provision of section 142 and 185(5) of the Companies Act 1948.

Mr S. Longson proposed:

'That Mr F. B. Walters, having attained the age of 70 years, be, and is hereby re-elected as Ordinary Director of the Company'.

Mr W. Ling seconded the resolution, which was put to the Meeting, and was declared carried.

Mr S. Longson proposed:

'That Mr F. B. Walters, Vice-President, retiring under paragraph 77(b) of the Company's Articles of Association be, and is hereby re-elected a Vice-President of the Company'.

Mr H. Cott seconded the resolution, which was put to the Meeting, and was carried.

Mr S. Longson proposed:

'That Mr T. W. Rudd, Director, retiring under paragraph 77(c) of the Company's Articles of Association be, and is hereby re-elected a Director of the Company'.

Mr R. Joell seconded the resolution, which was put to the Meeting, and was declared carried.

General

The Chairman addressed the Meeting and outlined the Club's policy in issuing further share capital. Discussion also took place in respect of the playing pitch and general spectator facilities on the Popular Side.

The Meeting closed with a vote of thanks to the Chairman, Board of Directors, Management and Playing Staff proposed by Mr L. Overton and seconded by Mr C. Cadman.

Editor's Comments

Frank Wignall joined Derby from Wolverhampton Wanderers for £20,000 in the latter stages of the Division Two championship-winning season, scoring on his debut as a substitute against Blackburn Rovers.

He was primarily deployed as a substitute, but also acted as cover for John O'Hare and Kevin Hector when either were injured or rested. In total he started 40 games, with a further 19 substitute appearances and scored 17 goals. His last appearance was against Crystal Palace on 6th November.

The release of Todd and Robson from the England Under-23 team to play Switzerland at Ipswich, together with the Hennessey and Durban's withdrawal from the Wales team to face Romania, meant that wholesale changes to the team and the very possibility of being beaten could be avoided in the Texaco Cup semi-final.

Annual General Meeting

The club's accounts showed a turnover of £345,386 and a profit of just £624 when they were published on 23rd October for the year ended 31st July 1971.

The transfer dealings (fees paid less fees received) taken into account were £170,390; the payments for Archie Gemmill and Colin Todd made up most of that amount with a small amount coming back from the outgoing transfers of Willie Carlin and Dave Mackay.

John McGovern and John Robson, with Alan Durban and Les Green (far right), show off the Watney Cup trophy to the Popside after beating Manchester United 4–1 in the Final, August 1970.

Dave Mackay leaves the field to waiting photographers at the final whistle after his last match for Derby against West Bromwich Albion, April 1971.

The Board of Directors (left to right):
(standing) Michael Keeling, Bill Rudd,
Sydney Bradley; (seated) Sir Robertson
King, Sam Longson (Chairman) and
Fred Walters.

Frank Innes, July 1970.

Derby break the transfer record for Colin Todd from Sunderland. Pictured: Sir Robertson King, Peter Taylor, Colin Todd, Sydney Bradley, Brian Clough and Michael Keeling. Missing was Sam Longson, who was away on holiday.

The telegram received by Sam Longson in the West Indies, where he was unaware of the transfer or fee involved.

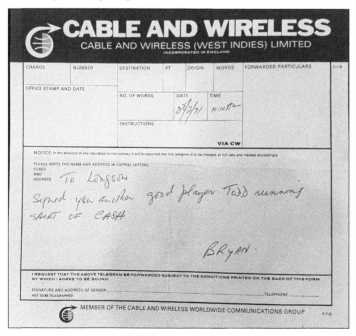

*The innovative newspaper/programme **The Ram**, a unique innovation of Stuart Webb, is launched by the club in July 1971, in readiness for a friendly against Schalke.*

Some of the Directors celebrate, after the last round of matches confirm that Derby are Champions of England for the first time.

Brian Clough with the Football League Championship trophy.

The players return to a packed Baseball Ground on Sunday 15th May to be presented with the Championship trophy and to receive their medals. Roy McFarland and Colin Todd missed the presentation as they were away on England duty.

Secretary Stuart Webb in his office surrounded by the three trophies: the Championship trophy, the Central League and the Texaco Cup.

David Nish breaks the British transfer record by signing from Leicester City, watched by Brian Clough, for a fee of £225,000.

The players in relaxed mood with a Greek newspaper reporter at Moor Lane sports ground, after training ahead of the Juventus European Cup semi-final match – Clough, Nish, Hector, McFarland and Davies.

The players return to a packed Baseball Ground on Sunday 15ᵗʰ May to be presented with the Championship trophy and to receive their medals. Roy McFarland and Colin Todd missed the presentation as they were away on England duty.

Sam Longson welcomes Dave Mackay back to the Baseball Ground, with the Derby Evening Telegraph reporting 'The Clough Saga is over'.

The money generated from football operations (£95,909) and Derby County Promotions (£77,000) allowed the club to pay for all of the upgrade in stadium facilities (new seats in the Middle Tier of the Osmaston Stand, the Sportsman's Club, toilets, bars, and new entrances and exits on the Pop Side) without further Bank borrowings.

In other highlights from the accounts:

Season ticket sales for the 1970–71 season	£175,019
Gate Receipts (less League %, and visiting club %)	£140,090
Programmes, Broadcasting, etc.	£18,047
Players and staff salaries	£129,330

One member of staff was in the £10,000–£12,500 salary bracket

The Directors' shareholding on 31st July 1971 was:

Sir Robertson King, KBE	50
S. Longson	110
F. B. Walters	235
S. C. Bradley	156
T. W. Rudd	10
F. W. Innes	10
M. Keeling	10

The agenda for the meeting was run through without undue delay, which is generally a sign the shareholders were giving a vote of confidence in the way in which the club and its administration was being run.

The Chairman gave an address at the end of the meeting that covered a number of topics, but explained that they were at a crossroads.

He explained, 'This town can support a First Division club, to say otherwise is tripe, but we are missing four or five thousand fans who we would expect to be here. Against Tottenham and Arsenal, for instance, we were that short of a capacity crowd when we expected to be closing the turnstiles.' In regards to the stadium, there was much to be done – redevelopment of the Normanton Stand, the Sinfin training ground, re-laying of the playing surface and upgrading the floodlights. The issue of how to finance the stadium costs and potential expensive player signings had to be balanced and ideas of how to raise that money were being investigated, which included a share issue and increases in ticket prices.

He said, 'as regards transfer fees, if you want success then you must pay the market price. But we have sound credentials, and will always try to spend wisely. Derby County have not gone bust, are not going bust and will not go bust.' He also recognised that better players (demanding large bonuses) would inevitably bring in greater receipts via the turnstiles allowing further re-investment in the infrastructure and players.

Internationally, O'Hare and Gemmill were selected in the Scotland squad to play a friendly against Holland in Amsterdam, whilst Graham Moseley and left-back Alan Lewis were in the England Youth squad to play Wales in Cardiff.

Thursday 25th November 1971

Prior to the meeting it was proposed by Mr S. C. Bradley, seconded by Sir Robertson King and unanimously agreed that Mr S. Longson be and is hereby re-elected Chairman of the company for a further period of one year.

Minute 6704 Manager's Report

The Manager, Mr B. H. Clough reported on relevant team matters during the past fortnight. It was agreed to change the date of our home Central League game at Christmas with Leeds United to Tuesday 28th December 1971. Kick-off 3.00 p.m.

Minute 6705 Floodlighting

A lengthy discussion took place regarding the condition of the Floodlights. The Television authorities had requested permission to install additional lighting to boost their picture quality. It was agreed to allow BBC Television to install their extra lighting provided it did not interefere with the players' vision. The Chairman proposed that up to date tenders be obtained from the lighting specialists with a view to the installing of a new floodlighting system during the close season.

Minute 6706 Texaco

Following the televising of our home Semi-Final Texaco Cup game with Newcastle United it was agreed the Secretary contact Texaco with regard to the gentleman's agreement between the two companies in respect of extra payment for additional TV coverage.

Minute 6707 Balance at Bank

The Company's overdrawn position at the Bank stood at £12,000. The Semi-Final cash gate of £10,000 not being included to date.

Editor's Comments

It was announced that the club would fly out to Athens and play a friendly against one of the leading Greek teams, Olympiakos Pireaus, on 14th December, who were managed by former West Bromwich Albion Manager Alan Ashman. The 20-strong party would be without Manager Clough, opting to leave Peter Taylor in charge of team affairs.

Tommy Docherty, the new Scotland Team Manager, paid a visit to see Brian Clough to discuss the international future of John McGovern, possibly including him in the squad to face England at the Baseball Ground in February.

Thursday 9th December 1971

ADDITION TO APPOINTMENT OF CHAIRMAN

Following the appointment of S. Longson as Chairman for the ensuing year, Mr F. W. Innes thanked Mr Longson on behalf of the Junior Directors for his guidance and friendliness during the past year.

Minute 6709 Manager's Report

Mr Peter Taylor, Assistant Manager reported on the relevant team matters and the Club's present injury position.

Dates for the Texaco Cup Final with Airdrie were confirmed as follows:

Airdrie v. Derby County – Wednesday 26th January 1972 7.30 p.m.

Derby County v. Airdrie – Wednesday 8th March 1972 7.30 p.m.

The Secretary confirmed that the League game with Leeds United at Elland Road on 27th December, 1971 would be all-ticket.

Minute 6710 Proposed New Normanton Stand

The Secretary reported that planning permission had been approved in respect of the Club's proposed development at the Normanton End of the Ground. Discussion took place regarding the proposed closure of Vulcan Street and it was reported that Derby Corporation were at present preparing the necessary legislation for the operation.

It was agreed that as an alternative to a new Stand, extra seats would be situated in the Normanton Stand. It was also agreed that preliminary plans be at hand in the event of an early decision.

Minute 6711 Balance at Bank

The Club's balance at the Bank stood at £8,000 overdrawn. Derby County Promotions having donated a further £5,000.

Minute 6712 Television at the Baseball Ground

Confirmation was received that the following games would be covered by ITV during the Month of January 1972.

Saturday 1st January 1972 v. Chelsea 3.00 p.m.

Minute 6714 Chelsea FC 1ˢᵗ January 1972

It was agreed that an invitation be extended to the Chelsea Board of Directors to attend a pre-match luncheon at the Midland Hotel prior to the game on 1ˢᵗ January 1972.

Minute 6715 Staff Pension Scheme

The Secretary outlined details of the proposed Staff Pension Scheme which would operate in respect of all Male Administrative Staff not already participating in the Football League Scheme. Annual Premiums in respect of P. Thorpe and M. Dunford would amount to £28 respectively.

Editor's Comments

There was an approach from the South American champions, Nacional Montevideo of Uruguay to play a friendly on Friday 18ᵗʰ December. They were contesting the World Club Championship and had just drawn 1–1 with Panathinaikos in Athens in the first leg and wanted to play another game before heading home. Being a Friday, it obviously had to be refused.

The Derby team flew out to Athens on Sunday 12ᵗʰ December for a four-day break that featured a match against Olympiakos Pireaus on the following Tuesday, the 14ᵗʰ. Peter Taylor managed a party of 13 players that included Peter Daniel and Jeff Bourne and said beforehand, 'we have come here to win'. The Greeks were managed by Alan Ashman, and were in second place in the Greek league behind Panathanaikos (managed by Puskas).

John Robson was back in action as they slipped to a 1–3 defeat and Taylor was pleased that his players did not react to some rather blatant obstruction and fouls committed by the home team. Being 0–3 down at half-time there was a much better performance in the second half, which they dominated, but they only had a single headed goal from John O'Hare to show for it.

David Miller in *The Times* wrote that Derby would have gained three valuable lessons in advance of any European matches next season:

1. Should not underestimate the opposition, regardless of the nationality. 'Derby looked bewildered rather as if they had been told they were to play Nuneaton and found themselves up against Manchester United.'

2. Should be aware that foreign referees may interpret the laws of the game differently and players should be wary.

3. Lack of strength in depth could be a problem when injuries and suspensions take effect. Colin Todd was absent due to a broken nose, and was badly missed.

With half of the League fixtures completed, Derby had relied upon just 14 players, one of those being the recently transferred Frank Wignall, and the other being 16-year-old Steve Powell, who had made just one senior start. Two apprentices were signed as new professionals – Alan Lewis (an England Youth International) and David Toon.

Friday 31st December 1971

Minute 6717 Manager's Report

The Manager, Mr B. H. Clough reported on relevant team matters and that an offer of £2,500 in respect of Jeff Bourne from Lincoln City had been refused.

It was agreed that a further contract for a period of three years be drawn up in respect of Trainer/Coach Jimmy Gordon.

A salary of   £2,600 from 1st January 1972 to 31st December 1972

                  £2,860 from 1st January 1973 to 31st December 1973

                  £3,120 from 1st January 1974 to 31st December 1974

Minute 6718 Proposed New Stand

It was reported that a meeting with Bass Worthington would be held on Wednesday 5th January 1972 to open discussions in connection with proposals for licenced premises to be included in the New Stand Structure.

Minute 6719 Balance at Bank

The Club's overdrawn position at the Bank stood at £15,000 to date. A further donation of £5,000 having been received from Derby County Promotions.

Minute 6721 Television at the Baseball Ground

Confirmation was recorded of ATV coverage of our FA Cup third-round tie v. Shrewsbury Town on Saturday 15th January 1972.

A fee of £87.50 would be receivable.

Minute 6722 Ground Staff Salary Increases

The following increases for Ground Staff personnel were confirmed to take effect from 1st January 1972:

H. Brown   £3 increase per week

A. Cleaver   £2 increase per week

B. Clough   £1 increase per week

G. Fletcher   £1 increase per week

R. Smith   £2 increase per week

R. Martin   £3 increase per week

Ram Editor

D. Moore   £4 increase per week

Coaching and Training Staff

J. Gordon £5 increase per week (to fall in line with new contract)

G. Guthrie £5 increase per week

J. Sheridan £5 increase per week

It was confirmed that the administrative staff salaries would be reviewed on 1st June 1972.

Minute 6723 Texaco Cup Staff Bonuses

The following bonuses in respect of the Texaco Cup Final were confirmed:

A. S. Webb £200   B. H. Clough £1,250

J. R. Howarth £100   P. Taylor £1,250

Minute 6724 Secretary

The Chairman raised the matter of a Contract of Service in respect of the Secretary. After general discussion it was agreed the matter be discussed further at a later date.

Thursday 13th January 1972

Before signing the Minutes of the previous meeting the Chairman passed a proposition which was unanimously agreed that Minute 6722 in respect of Contract of Service for James Gordon be rescinded. The Chairman on behalf of the Board undertook to discuss the financial matter further with the Manager.

Minute 6726 Manager's Report

The Manager, Mr B. H. Clough reported on relevant team matters during the past week.

A request from Burton Albion FC to purchase our existing floodlights should the Club purchase new ones was considered along with the possibility of a pre-season friendly game regarding the transfer agreement between our two Clubs in respect of Anthony Bailey. It was agreed the matter be discussed at a later date. Preliminary plans were being drawn up in respect of the Club's pre-season 1972–73 Tour. The Manager proposed a tour of Holland taking in three games with leading Dutch opposition.

Minute 6727 Balance at Bank

The Club's overdrawn Balance at the Bank to date stood at £20,000. A further donation of £5,000 having been received from Derby County Promotions.

Minute 6728 Anglo–Italian Competition 1972

It was confirmed that the Club had refused an invitation from the Football League to take part in the summer's Anglo–Italian Competition.

Minute 6729 Under-23 International at Derby 16th February 1972

The Secretary outlined details in respect of the proposed International game. A pre-match reception for Sportsman's Club Members and VIPs would be sponsored by Bells Scotch Whisky and commence at 6.00 p.m. Following the game The Mayor of Derby invited Players, Officials and Derby County Directors to a Civic Reception and Buffet in the Council House commencing at 10.00 p.m.

The Secretary confirmed that he would be attending meetings at the Football Association's Headquarters during the early part of February in respect of this game.

The Board of Directors wished the Chairman all best wishes in respect of his forthcoming holiday. The Chairman proposed that during his absence Mr S. C. Bradley take over the duties of Chairman in respect of Board Meetings. This proposition was seconded by Sir Robertson King and unanimously agreed.

Prior to the Board Meeting, a meeting with Mr Haines of Mosby, Haines Partnership took place in respect of the proposed new Stand. The Chairman instructed Mr Haines to proceed with preliminary discussions with Derby Corporation and Bass Worthington in order that a decision could be taken in the near future.

Confirmation had been received that Derby Corporation had approved Plans for a new Stand and agreed to progress with legislation to the eventual closure of Vulcan Street.

Friday 28th January 1972

Minute 6731 Manager's Report

The Manager, Mr B. H. Clough reported on the Club's injury position and of the probable team to play against Coventry City.

It was agreed that a donation of £25 be forwarded to Shirebrook FC in respect of the Club having recently signed David Toon on Professional Forms.

An invitation from Lincoln City to take part in a five-a-side competition during the month of July was declined.

Minute 6732 TV Coverage v. Notts County

After a lengthy discussion it was agreed that the Club refuse permission to have the Cup tie v. Notts County televised by ATV. It was agreed that in principle the Club had been over exposed recently and that the fee offered of £87.50 was totally inadequate. The Secretary would notify both the FA and ATV accordingly.

Minute 6733 Texaco

The Secretary reported on a Meeting in Airdrie with M. Slaughter of Texaco in respect of payment over the existing contract with Texaco in regard to additional coverage on television. It was agreed that the offer from Texaco be accepted.

Texaco Semi-Final v. Newcastle United November 1971 £600 (confirmed)

Texaco Cup Final v. Airdrie 8th March 1972 £600 (if televised)

Under-23 International England v. Scotland 16th February £800 (if televised)

Minute 6734 Balance at Bank

The Club's overdrawn Balance at the Bank stood at £26,000, £4,500 having been received from Texaco in respect of Rounds 1, 2 and Semi-Final of the Texaco Cup.

Minute 6735 Under-23 International England v. Scotland

It was confirmed that Sir Robertson King, Mr F. B. Walters and Mr S. C. Bradley would attend an official reception at the Midland Hotel at 5.00 p.m. on Wednesday 16th February 1972 prior to the game at the Baseball Ground.

Editor's Comments

The club refused permission for the FA Cup match against Notts County to be shown on the ATV network on the Sunday afternoon highlights programme. There were two main reasons why this refusal occurred:

1. The facility fee. The third-round match against Shrewsbury Town, also shown on an ATV highlights programme, saw a facility cheque arrive from the Football Association for just £87.50. The FA had negotiated a television deal and the money from that was evenly distributed amongst all the clubs playing in that round, with a bigger share going to the clubs actually shown on TV. The facility fee was thought not to be high enough to warrant the disruption caused by the TV crews for three days and loss of capacity when additional scaffolding and cameras were installed.

2. Over-exposure. During the two and a half years since they were promoted to the First Division they had been on TV at total of 56 times; 21 in 1969–70, 20 in 1970–71 and 15 so far in 1971–72. For this particular tie, Billy Wright (former England captain and Head of Sport) said it was their first choice being a local derby and with Derby always attracting an above-average TV audience. The fees were negotiated at the beginning of the season with the Football Association, so little could be done.

Tony Parry, a 26-year-old defender, a recent signing from Hartlepool United, made his debut in midfield during the Texaco Cup Final at Airdrie, which was quite a physical tie, with the Scottish League referees using a more lenient interpretation of the rules. A 0–0 draw gave Derby a good chance of winning the competition with the home leg to come. Parry was well known to the management, having been with Peter Taylor at Burton Albion and then again at Hartlepool and could play in any of the defensive positions as well as midfield.

Brian Clough enraged the Professional Footballers Association by banning the Derby players from giving evidence at disciplinary hearings in support of opponents. Colin Todd had recently given evidence in support of Manchester City's Francis Lee, who successfully appealed against a booking. Clough had since turned down an approach from Manchester

United to support Dennis Law, and said, 'everybody will get that answer from now on'.

Thursday 10ᵗʰ February 1972

Minute 6737 Manager's Report

Mr P. Taylor, the Assistant Manager reported to the Meeting the probable teams for Saturday and the Club's present injury position.

Confirmation had been received from the Football League regarding two end of season fixtures that clashed with England European Competitions.

New Dates:

Wednesday 22ⁿᵈ March 1972 Derby County v. Ipswich Town

Monday 1ˢᵗ May 1972 Derby County v. Liverpool

The Manager, Mr B. H. Clough came into the meeting and discussion took place regarding the senior management and administrative structure of the Club. After a lengthy discussion it was agreed to leave the matter until the Club Chairman, Mr S. Longson returned from holiday.

Minute 6738 Under-23 International

The Secretary reported on his recent visit to the Football Association in connection with the International England v. Scotland.

Due to power cuts the kick-off would now be 2.30 p.m. BBC Television would cover the game and a fee of £800 would be payable to Derby County by the FA. The Mayoral Reception would now be held at 7.00 p.m. at The Council House, Derby on Tuesday 15ᵗʰ February 1972.

Minute 6739 Balance at Bank

The Club's overdrawn balance at the Bank stood at £25,000. A further donation of £5,000 having been received from Derby County Promotions.

Minute 6740 FA Cup Fifth Round v. Arsenal

The Secretary confirmed arrangements for the Club's all-ticket game with Arsenal to be held on Saturday 26th February 1972.

A home tie of this nature ensured that all four Season ticket Cup Vouchers would now be needed.

Minute 6741 Club Chairmen Meeting, Monday 7th February 1972

Mr S. C. Bradley reported on the Football League's Chairmen's Meeting held in London. Many general topics being covered and discussed with a view to streamlining and presenting to the League's AGM during the summer.

Minute 6742 Scottish Football Association

It was confirmed that the Club would not be in a position to release John O'Hare and Archie Gemmill for Scottish International duties during the months of June/July 1972.

Minute 6743 W. Stevenson

It was agreed a letter of appreciation be sent to Mr W. Stevenson in respect of his gift to the Sportsmen's Club of a heated door screen.

Editor's Comments

There was a fixture problem caused by the England v. West Germany European Nations Cup match that was to be played on Saturday 29th April. This meant that all matches scheduled for that date, and earlier in that week had to be rearranged, with the new date for the Liverpool game originally set as Wednesday 3rd May. With the FA Cup Final to be played on the following Saturday, and Derby still in the competition at the sixth-round stage, having to play Liverpool on the 3rd and a potential Cup Final on the 6th did not fit very well, so the fixture was moved to Monday evening. The League was also to allow the eventual Cup finalists to move their fixtures from Cup Final week to the following week.

With the League setting a deadline date when all domestic fixtures had to be completed, there was the potential for a fixture pile-up with the Texaco Cup Final, scheduled for March 8th to play, the fifth-round FA Cup game against Arsenal meant that the League game at Crystal Palace was moved to following Tuesday evening, unless the Arsenal game was to go to a replay which would take priority. Three home Reserve games had been postponed, the game scheduled for the Arsenal Cup day and the away game at Blackburn Rovers all to be rearranged.

Saturday 19th February 1972

EMERGENCY BOARD MEETING

PRESENT:

Mr S. C. Bradley (In Chair)

Sir Robertson King, KBE

Mr F. B. Walters

Mr T. W. Rudd

Mr F. W. Innes

Mr M. Keeling

IN ATTENDANCE:

Mr A. S. Webb, Secretary

Mr B. H. Clough, Manager

An apology for absence was received from Chairman, Mr S. Longson.

Minute 6745 Television Coverage, FA Fifth Round Cup Tie,
Saturday 26th February 1972

Mr S. C. Bradley outlined the purpose of the Meeting to the Board. The Football Association had requested that the Club reconsider its decision to ban TV coverage of the FA Cup game with Arsenal. After a lengthy discussion in which many views were expressed including the Manager's views on not wishing the game to be televised.

A proposition from Mr F. W. Innes, seconded by Mr M. Keeling was put to the Meeting:

'That the Board support the Manager in his request for no television coverage of the Cup tie providing this action did not contravene any Rules or Agreements made between the Football Association and the Television Authorities.'

An amendment to Mr Innes' proposition was put forward by Sir Robertson King and seconded by Mr F. B. Walters. 'That the Board accept the Football Association's offer on behalf of ATV to televise the Cup tie.'

The amendment was put to the Meeting first and defeated by three votes to two.

The proposition then being put to the Meeting was carried by three votes to two.

The Chairman did not vote.

It was agreed the Secretary inform the Football Association of the Board's decision.

Thursday 24th February 1972

Minute 6746 Manager's Report

The Manager, Mr B. H. Clough came into the Meeting and reported on general team matters and the probable team to play Arsenal in the FA Cup Fifth Round. Discussion took place regarding television coverage at the Baseball Ground and it was agreed that in principle the Club had no objections to TV coverage gernerally but would consider each individual case if and when it arose.

The Secretary raised the issue of a newspaper advertisement for Staff that had been placed by the Manager. A discussion took place regarding the Managerial structure of the Club and it was confirmed that until the present structure was changed, the Secretary was directly responsible to the Board of Directors for the Administration of the Club.

Minute 6747 Under-23s International at the Baseball Ground

A letter of appreciation was recorded from the Football Association in respect of the Club's recent organisation in staging the England v. Scotland International. It was proposed by Mr F. W. Innes and seconded by Mr T. W. Rudd that a vote of thanks be recorded in respect of the Secretary, Mr A. S. Webb's contribution toward making the occasion a huge success.

The Club had banked £3,000 profit after receiving the necessary percentage from the Football Association and TV Fees.

Minute 6748 Balance at Bank

The Club's overdrawn balance at the Bank stood at £29,088. A further £5,000 having been donated from Derby County Promotions. Donations to date totalled £40,000.

Minute 6749 Texaco Cup Final 8th March 1972

The Secretary outlined arrangements for the Cup Final with Airdrie. A pre-match meal would be held at the Midland Hotel at 5.00 p.m. when the Club would entertain VIPs from the Football League, Scottish League, Airdrieonians and Texaco.

Minute 6750 BBC Television

The Secretary confirmed that the Club would receive £865 in respect of use of the television gantry dating back from 19th September 1970 up to date. It had been agreed that for all future BBC visits the Club would receive £75 for the gantry and £25 for loss of spectator spaces.

Minute 6751 Esso Petroleum Limited

It was reported that the Club had received £500 through the Football League in respect of a Club Badge promotion at present being issued by Esso Limited.

Editor's Comments

The Arsenal captain, Frank McLintock had gone to the press ahead of the fifth-round FA Cup tie describing the Baseball Ground pitch as 'diabolical, a disgrace, ridiculous – a bumpy, terrible mudheap, unfit for football, and surely the worst in the First Division'. Whilst the club recognised there were issues, improvements to drainage and topsoil over the course of the summer had improved the situation and proof of that came in the last round against Notts County. The pitch, which was actually lying below street level, was under snow until midweek, followed by heavy rain on the Thursday and more before kick-off without a hint of a postponement. Clough responded, 'at Derby we pay our players to play football.'

Regardless of the condition of the pitch, the referee has the authority to postpone the game if he believes the conditions are unplayable or unsafe.

16th February 1972: The Under-23 International between England and Scotland took place at the Baseball Ground. With the threat of power cuts during this time, the game had been moved to a midweek afternoon which meant that many youngsters were denied the opportunity of seeing the future stars. Just over 18,000 fans saw the game and witnessed a 2–2 draw amongst worsening pitch conditions, a result of almost 36 hours of continuous rainfall. The Scottish Under-23 Manager, Tommy Docherty, said after the game, 'You wouldn't have asked horses to play out there let alone professional footballers,' and Bill Shankly said, 'You couldn't pass the ball on it, or even kick it more than a few yards.'

In preparation for the FA Cup tie, the pitch was covered by large plastic sheets which were then inflated by hot air blowers to create a 'tent', similar to one used at Leicester City. According to Clough, 'no method which could improve the playing surface should be ignored by any club.'

Following on from the Chairman's statement at the Annual General Meeting, the Manager reiterated and expanded on them by claiming that unless attendances were to increase to nearly 40,000 then the chances of top honours would be slim. With transfer fees increasing steadily he said, 'Derby County simply cannot compete as things stand. We just haven't the money. Unless we begin to attract several thousand more spectators – and what more can we do to bring them in? – we will have to make do as we are.' In terms of numbers, the average home attendance was 32,462 which was the 10th-best in the League, compared to 47,000 at Liverpool and Manchester United.

4th March: Derby had some 14,000 (one third) tickets to sell for the fifth-round FA Cup second replay game which was to be held at Filbert Street, Leicester on Monday 13th March. These would go on sale on the Thursday before the game, as the Texaco Cup Final was to be played on the evening beforehand.

Thursday 9th March 1972

Minute 6753 Manager's Report

The Assistant Manager, Mr P. Taylor was called into the Meeting and reported on relevant team matters. Discussion took place regarding Ian Moore's transfer from Nottingham Forest to Manchester United and the involvement of Derby County. It was confirmed that everything possible had been done to secure Moore's signature for Derby County but under strong pressure from Nottingham Forest they had persuaded him to sign for Manchester United. It was also confirmed that on two occasions the Club had asked the Football League to look into the matter but on both occasions had been refused on the grounds of the transfer being a domestic matter between two Clubs.

Minute 6754 TV Coverage v. Leeds United

It was confirmed that an invitation from the Football League for our home game on Easter Saturday v. Leeds United to be televised by the BBC had been received. After discussion it was agreed that permission be granted.

Minute 6755 Season tickets 1972–73

The Secretary outlined proposed increases in Season ticket prices for next Season. After a general discussion the following were confirmed:

	Single Match Price	21 Home League	Cost of Season ticket	Saving to Season ticket Holders
'B' Stand & Ley Centre	£1.25	£26.25	£20	£6.25
'A' & 'C' Stands & Ley Wings	£1	£21	£17	£4
Osmaston & Normanton Stand	80p	£16.80	£14	£2.80

Due to the success of the Cup Voucher system it was agreed to again include Four Cup Vouchers in the Season ticket Books.

Single match Admissions would be increased as follows:

Popular Side up from 30p to 35p.

Osmaston and Normanton Terracing up from 40p to 45p.

Children's Enclosure up from 15p to 20p.

OAPs up from 10p to 15p.

Minute 6756 Football League Championship 1st April 1972

It was confirmed that the home game on Easter Saturday versus Leeds United would be an 'All-Ticket Game'.

Minute 6757 Sportsmen's Club

Discussion took place in respect of Membership Fees for The Sportsman's Club for Season 1972–73. It was agreed that no prices would be given and Membership for 1972–73 Season would be single £15 – Man and wife £25.

It was also agreed that plans and drawings be prepared for a Clubroom along similar lines to be erected in Ley Stand.

Minute 6758 Balance at Bank

It was confirmed that the Club's overdrawn balance at the Bank stood at £22,000.

Minute 6759 Experimental Pitch Covering

Mr M. Keeling outlined details of an agreement with Mr I. McCleod, the Manager, in respect of a proposed pitch covering for the Baseball Ground. After due consideration and experience, it was agreed that the covering was not suitable for Derby County and the matter was left with Mr Keeling and the Secretary to finalise any payment owing to Mr McCleod and report back to the Board.

Minute 6760 Proposed New Stand

Mr F. W. Innes undertook to speak to Bass Charrington Limited in respect of a price being asked by them for the Baseball Hotel. Mosby Haines Partnership having indicated that both the Brewery and Leys Malleable Castings were prepared to negotiate regarding the Club's proposed new Normanton Development.

Editor's Comments

The Ian Moore transfer saga made front page news in the national newspapers as there was widespread confusion as to where the player would go to. As far as Derby were concerned, they had spoken to the 27-year-old player, agreed terms and all of the paperwork regarding the transfer had been completed, and were waiting for a signature from the Nottingham Forest end to complete the £200,000 deal. Moore himself thought he had signed and was staying in the Derby team hotel (Midland Hotel) and was paraded in front of the 33,456 fans on Saturday 4th March prior to the game against Wolverhampton Wanderers as a Derby player, and even made a press statement: 'Brian Clough's offer was too good to turn down. I am delighted it is Derby I have joined.' The other club in discussions at the same time was Manchester United, and his wife was set on a move to Manchester with both clubs having agreed terms, so the Derby link came as a bit of a surprise to everyone. The parading of Moore on the pitch had angered the Nottingham Forest committee and instead of ratifying the transfer, they promptly blocked it as they were angered by Clough's pressurising tactics. Within a couple of days Moore and Nottingham Forest had completed a deal with Manchester United and the Nottingham Forest Secretary, Ken Smales, said, 'Derby's behaviour in these negotiations has been unpleasant.'

No sooner had the Moore transfer been completed than the press were looking for Derby's next transfer target, and looked at who Moore would replace at Manchester United – George Best. Best was struggling with his form and with United having lost their last six games, changes were becoming inevitable.

The Texaco Cup Final, scheduled to be played on 8th March, was postponed. The pitch was heavy, but playable on Tuesday, but an overnight downpour completely changed the situation. By 8.30 a.m. on the day of the game it was unplayable and needed Jack Taylor from Wolverhampton to officially call a postponement and yet another fixture to re-arrange before the end of the season.

With seat Season tickets for season 1972–73 going on sale in May, supporters were urged to buy quickly as once outside the renewal period their ticket would be allocated to one of the several hundreds of names on the seat waiting list, a list that was growing at a rate of six per day.

March 22nd:

The recurring theme of the low attendances was raised again when just 26,738 fans attended the Ipswich Town match, the lowest of the season, some 6,000 below the average and 14,000 below capacity and the figure targeted by the Chairman and Manager to make the club competitive. The Manager told *The Ram*, 'It's depressing when the team is doing so well. There must be a reason the town is turning its back on us.' Stuart Webb commented, 'Income of this sort from the gate just isn't enough to do the sort of things the public expect from us.'

March 29th:

The Coventry City Chairman, Derek Robins, made an official approach to be able to speak to Clough and Taylor regarding the managerial vacancy at his club following the departure of Noel Cantwell, whilst the team were in the team hotel in the London area following their fixture at Crystal Palace. Permission was duly given and the management duly accepted the terms offered by Coventry. Longson would not allow them to leave immediately as Coventry had wanted with the end of the season so close.

April 1st:

The *Daily Express* had reported the Coventry City story, claiming that money was no object to get the right man. Clough distanced himself from these reports by saying, 'I'm on a five-year contract at Derby and it's got two and a half years to run. I fully expect to see it out. I'm not planning on going to Coventry. I'm not going anywhere. How could I leave Derby while we are so close to winning the championship?'

Thursday 13th April 1972

Minute 6762 Manager's Report

The Manager, Mr B. H. Clough reported on relevant team matters since the last meeting and of the probable team for Saturday's game with Stoke City.

Discussion took place regarding a proposed pre-season tour 1972–73. It was agreed that two games in Holland and one in Germany would be arranged during the period 23rd July 1972 and 3rd August 1972.

Minute 6763 Ground Improvements

The Chairman outlined proposals for ground improvements that would take place during the summer months. Mr Perks would be meeting the Chairman and Secretary in respect of the proposed additional seating in the Normanton Stand.

Minute 6764 Balance at Bank

The Club's overdrawn balance at the Bank stood at £31,333.

Minute 6765 I. McCleod

It was confirmed that an *ex gratia* payment of £250 would be paid to Mr I. McCloed in respect of his efforts and time in experimenting with a proposed pitch covering. It was reported that the Club would not be involved in further developments of this nature.

Minute 6765 Floodlighting

The Secretary confirmed that following the Meeting, Members of the Board would meet representatives of Phillips Electrical with regard to new Floodlights.

Friday 14th April 1972

Minute 6767 Manager's Report

Both the Manager and Assistant Manager were absent from the Meeting due to being away, with the Team at Scarborough in preparation for Saturday's game with Sheffield United.

Minute 6768 Single Match Prices 1972–73

It was agreed that following the Football League Directive that the minimum admission charge for 1972–73 would be increased to 40p the admission charges would be:

Osmaston/Normanton Terraces 50p

Paddock	50p
Popular Side	40p
Children's Pen	25p
0AP	20p

It was also agreed that the possibilities of a pen for Season ticket Holders on the Popular Side be looked into.

Minute 6769 Club Newspaper - The Ram

Discussion took place regarding proposals for production of *The Ram* as a Club Newspaper for next Season. It was agreed that the newspaper had been a success and that a guarantee of £10,000 from the publishers would be acceptable for Season 1972–73. The matter of negotiations was left to Mr Keeling and the Secretary.

Minute 6770 Balance at Bank

The Club's overdrawn balance at the Bank stood at £21,500 to date.

Minute 6771 Normanton Additional Seats

It was proposed by Mr F. W. Innes and seconded by Mr T. W. Rudd that an additional 1,200 seats be added to the Lower Deck of Normanton Stand at a cost of £9,200 during the Close Season.

Minute 6772 Share Transfer

The following share transfer was confirmed and saw certificates signed:

Archer/Robotham/Jeffries to J. Kirkland, Belper   2,434 shares

---

Editor's Comments

Commenting upon the recently released Season ticket prices for the 1972–73 season, which was hoped would bring in £300,000, the Chairman commented, 'We have heard quite a bit about disappointing attendances this season … and we've also been told, frequently, that the stadium still has spectator comfort deficiencies. But which comes first? We are told that more support is guaranteed to us when the Baseball Ground is further improved. Yet we could do with that support NOW to boost the funds available for doing the job.'

Manager Clough once again was critical of the fans, or lack of them. Not for the first time during the season, it had been commented upon by not only the Manager, but also the Board at how disappointed they were in the attendances and that the Club should expect more fans coming through the gate. In the case of the Huddersfield Town game on 15th April, the attendance was 31,000 with the ground capacity being nearly 40,000. It would be expected that the crowd should be around the 35,000 mark to watch a team on a good run of form, top of the First Division and with a real possibility of winning the championship.

The attendances, it was speculated, may also have a future impact on Clough's decision to stay or go to another club with bigger crowd potential.

26th April: The rearranged Texaco Cup Final took place against Airdrieonians some seven weeks after the original game had been scheduled. Despite the large number of matches played since that time, the original *Ram* newspaper/programme was issued on the night.

Both Roy McFarland (groin strain) and Colin Todd (ankle) failed fitness tests ahead of England's Nations Cup (forerunner to the European Championships) quarter-final, first leg match against West Germany at Wembley Stadium on Saturday and both would already be doubts for Monday's final game. McFarland's place would likely go to Liverpool's Larry Lloyd, who would probably be in the Liverpool squad to play at Derby just 48 hours later.

Newspaper reports continued to suggest that Coventry City were to appoint Brian Clough and Peter Taylor as their new management team on a joint contract worth £40,000 annually.

Thursday 27th April 1972

Minute 6774 Balance at Bank
The Club's overdrawn balance at the Bank stood at £14,500 overdrawn.

Minute 6775 Floodlighting

It was confirmed that following the Meeting, discussion would take place with representatives from Thorn Electrical in respect of proposed new Floodlighting at the Baseball Ground.

Minute 6776 Playing Pitch

The Chairman confirmed that acting on a report from Dr Adams of Aberystwyth University. A large quantity of sand would be applied to the playing surface during the Close Season. It was agreed that casual labour be employed to assist with the operation.

Minute 6777 Share Transfer

H. Payne to J. Kirkland, Belper   370 shares

Minute 6778 A. J. Parry

It was agreed subject to Football League approval to loan A. J. Parry the sum of £450 in respect of house purchase.

Minute 6779 Manager's Report

The Manager, Mr B. H. Clough came into the Meeting and reported that Robson and Todd would not be taking part in the FA Under-23s Close Season Tour. It was agreed the Secretary prepare necessary letters on their behalf and to notify the Football Association.

It was reported that C. Boulton had been fined £20 in respect of a breach of Club discipline.

The Manager reported that he would be leaving the Club following our last home game on 1st May and would take up employment as Manager of Coventry City on 2nd May 1972. It was confirmed that P. Taylor, Assistant Manager and J. Gordon, Trainer/Coach would also be leaving the Club.

After a lenghty discussion in which several propositions were put forward, it was agreed with regret that the Board accept the the three resignations.

It was agreed that the Club's Solicitors examine the Contracts of Service of the three employees in respect of a possible breach of contract.

Editor's Comments

At the same time as the Board Meeting was taking place, Coventry City had sent their Assistant Secretary, Mr Dennison, who was en route to Derby with a letter formally withdrawing their offer to the management duo and Jimmy Gordon. Stuart Webb was told by Mr Dennison late in the afternoon about the contents and this was delivered to Clough at home.

Clough, Taylor and Director Michael Keeling went to Longson's house that evening to suggest that they would stay on if Derby would pay them more money. This amounted to quite a substantial increase and would be ratified at an Emergency Board Meeting that would be held the following morning, with Longson not yet aware of the full picture.

Webb, not being aware of the evening meeting, did not tell Longson about the Coventry letter until the morning and Longson was hugely annoyed that he had been deceived in this way.

Jack Kirkland continued to buy up any shares coming to the market and was fortunate to acquire two thirds of the shares owned by former Chairman, the late Oswald Jackson. This, along with the other share dealings, made him the second-largest shareholder.

Friday 28ᵗʰ April 1972

SPECIAL BOARD MEETING

PRESENT: Mr S. Longson (Chairman)

Sir Robertson King, KBE

Mr F. B. Walters

Mr S. C. Bradley

Mr T. W. Rudd

Mr F. W. Innes

Mr M. Keeling

IN ATTENDANCE: Mr A. S. Webb, Secretary

Discussion took place regarding a further Contract of Service for a further five years in respect of the Manager and Assistant Manager.

Following detailed discussions with the Manager and Assistant Manager it was confirmed that the terms outlined below had been accepted by the Manager and Assistant Manager following discussions at the Chairman's home on the previous evening when the Manager and Assistant Manager agreed to stay with the Club and not go to Coventry City subject to receiving the following new Contract with increased terms of £5,000 and £3,000 per annum respectively.

B. H. CLOUGH

A 5-year contract commencing 1st May 1972.

Salary £14,000

Insurance £ 1,000

£15,000 per annum

No Company Car would be provided but travelling expenses of 10p per mile were confirmed.

P. TAYLOR

A 5-year contract commencing 1st May 1972.

Salary £8,000 per annum.

A Company Car to be provided.

The following incentives were confirmed to cover the period of Contract:

Football League

1st in Football League Division One £5,000 each

2nd in Football League Division One £3000

3rd, 4th, 5th, 6th in Football League Division One £2,000

7th, 8th in Football League Division One £500

FA Cup

£5,000 each for reaching the Cup Final

£3,000 each for reaching the Semi-final

£1500 each for reaching the Sixth Round

£1000 each for reaching the Fifth Round

£500 each for reaching the Fourth Round

Football League Cup

£5,000 for reaching Cup Final (each)

£3,000 for reaching Semi-final (each)

£1,500 for reaching Sixth Round

£1,000 for reaching Fifth Round

£500 for reaching Fourth Round

Editor's Comments

It was planned that the announcement that Clough and Taylor would be staying at Derby would be released on Monday morning, the day of their last and probably decisive League game against Liverpool. Sam Longson told one reporter on Friday night, 'Yes, we have had the meeting. Yes, Brian Clough is staying at Derby. They have agreed to sign new contracts for five years.'

Colin Todd was named as the Derby County Player of the Year as voted for by the supporters. He beat captain Roy McFarland into second place and Archie Gemmill in third.

Derby's Reserve team had clinched the Central League title by winning their last home game against Coventry City (4–3) and still had two away matches to play at Liverpool and Leeds United. This latest victory in front of a crowd of 5,300 stretched the unbeaten run to 21 games and meant that goalkeeper Graham Moseley had not been on a losing side since he joined the club in late September.

Monday 1ˢᵗ May 1972:

16-year-old Steve Powell, who had previously made only two appearances for the Club, was called into the First team for one of the title-deciding matches, replacing the injured Ron Webster. Clough was full of praise for the youngster: 'It would not matter whether he was only 14 as long as I thought he had the ability. He has played some fabulous games in the Reserves so I don't see any reason why I should not bring him in as a direct swap for Webster.'

On the same evening as the Derby v. Liverpool match, the title favourites, Leeds United were also in action, beating Chelsea 2–0, with the following morning's papers dominated by Leeds and installed as 3-1 on for the title with the bookmakers with Derby at 5-1 and Liverpool 7-1, with Liverpool having to beat Arsenal at Highbury and Leeds only needing a point at Wolverhampton Wanderers the following Monday.

Thursday 4ᵗʰ May 1972:

Derby's squad flew out to Majorca for a 10-day holiday, with Roy McFarland and Colin Todd heading back to the UK on Monday to join up with the England squad to play West Germany in the second leg of the Nations Cup and Home Internationals.

Tuesday 9ᵗʰ May 1972:

The previous evening's results (a 0–0 draw between Arsenal and Liverpool and a 2–1 defeat for Leeds United) meant that Derby were champions of the Football League for the first time in their history, winning by a point. Manager Clough was away on a family holiday in Tresco in the Scilly Isles and the players were in Majorca. On hearing the final scores, a number of people were asked their feelings:

Brian Clough – '*I don't feel sorry for Don Revie. The Derby players have done so well and done so much they have earned the championship.*'

Kevin Hector – '*Our courier said you look like a bunch of expectant fathers. How true that was. We've all given birth to the League crown.*'

Archie Gemmill – '*This is the greatest thing that's ever happened to me in football.*'

Alan Durban – '*We are all over the moon – and there's a big one shining here tonight.*'

John Robson – '*We had been living in hope since we arrived here and now it's all come true, it's just too much.*'

Alan Hinton – '*This is the moment we've been waiting for especially for me after 10 years in the game.*'

Tuesday 16th May 1972

Minute 6781 Manager's Report

The Chairman, on behalf of the Board of Directors congratulated the Management on the wonderful achievement of winning the Championship of the Football League.

Discussion took place regarding Colin Todd and John Robson seeking their release from England's Under-23 close season Tour.

It was agreed the matter be left with the players and that the Secretary notify the Football Association accordingly.

Minute 6782 Balance at Bank

The Club's credit balance at the Bank stood at £77,000 to date. An estimated £50,000 being due for payment in respect of bonuses outstanding to players and management winning the Football League Championship.

Minute 6782 Season tickets 1972–73

Season ticket sales to date in respect of Season 1972–73 stood at £102,000.

Minute 6783 Floodlighting

Following a special meeting of the Board on Tuesday 9th May 1972 in respect of a new Floodlighting system it was confirmed that a quotation from Thorn Electrics in conjunction with Christy Electrical Ltd be accepted. The price being £30,859.78.

Completion date for the contract being 22nd July 1972.

Minute 6784 Administrative Staff

The following salary increases in respect of the administration were agreed with effect from 1st May 1972.

J. R. Howarth	£3.50 per week	Promotions Staff	
P. Thorpe	£3	Mrs Hair	£2 per week
J. A. Glenn	£3	A. Cross	£2
M. Dunford	£2.50	P. A. Henry	£2
L. Hancock	£2.50	M. O'Sullivan	£2
		Mrs Jennings	£1.50

Thursday 8th June 1972

Minute 6786 Manager's Report

The Manager, Mr B. H. Clough came into the meeting and reported on relevant team matters.

Two players McGovern and Mason had accepted new contracts, Gemmill had been offered an increase of £5 per week to £85 per week but to date had not yet signed. McFarland would be having discussions during the course of the next few days following the meeting.

It was confirmed that the Club would not be accepting the Football Association's invitation to take part in the Charity Shield on Saturday 5th August 1972. The Cup

Winners, Leeds Utd, had also asked to be excused.

Salary increases in respect of the following Groundstaff were confirmed:

R. Smith £1 per week

R. Martin £1 per week

B. Clough £1 per week

A. Cleaver £1 per week

Minute 6787 Pre-Season Tour of Holland & Germany

The Secretary outlined details of the pre-season tour as follows:

Sunday 23rd July 1972 Depart Derby

Tuesday 25th July 1972 A.D.O. v. Derby County 8.00 p.m.

Saturday 29th July 1972 Tilburg FC v. Derby County 3.00 p.m.

Tuesday 1st August 1972 Schalke 04 v. Derby County 8.00 p.m.

Thursday 3rd August 1972 Party returns to England.

Saturday 5th August 1972 Derby County v. A.D.O. 7.30p.m.

Total fees for the trip amounted to approximately £8,000.00. It was agreed that the team coach would be used by the party whilst on the Continent. The main party would travel by air.

Minute 6788 Sinfin Sports Ground

It was reported that vandals had caused extensive damage to Dressing Rooms at Sinfin. It was agreed that additional fencing be erected to protect the field and dressing room areas.

Minute 6789 Balance at Bank

It was reported that the Club's credit balance at the Bank to date stood at £126,000.

Minute 6790 Season tickets 1972–73

Season tickets Sales in respect of the Season 1972–73 stood at £240,000.

Minute 6791 County Civic Reception

It was confirmed that the County Civic Reception would be held at Matlock on Tuesday 18th July 1972.

Minute 6792 Championship Dinner

It was confirmed that the Championship Dinner would be held at the Pennine Hotel on Friday 21st July 1972 for 350 Guests.

Minute 6793 National Westminster Bank Limited

Following discussion with the Bank in respect of Directors' signatures on Company Cheques it was agreed that in order to establish a more convenient working arrangement in future the Secretary and one Director's signature would be adequate on all Company cheques.

Minute 6793a The Ram

The Secretary outlined proposals in respect of the official Club Newspaper for Season 1972–73. Cartmell Publications' offer of £8,000.00 was inadequate and it was agreed to handle the Publication of the Newspaper from within the framework of the Club. With this venture in mind it was agreed that a suitable Advertising/ Circulation Manager be sought to increase revenue and to assist with Sponsoram.

Minute 6794 New Floodlighting System

Discussion took place regarding possible excessive payment of between £2,000 and £3,000 in respect of additional foundation work. Following a report from Mr F. W. Innes it was agreed to leave the matter with the Chairman and Secretary to resolve.

Minute 6795 Proposed New Stand

Mr F. W. Innes reported on further talks with Bass Worthington Ltd, in respect of purchasing the Baseball Hotel and it was agreed every effort be made to come to terms with the Brewery at the earliest convenience.

Minute 6796 Championship Bonuses

The following bonuses in respect of the Club winning the 1st Division Championship were agreed to be paid to:

A. S. Webb, Secretary　　　　　　£650.00

J. Howarth, Assistant Secretary　£100.00

Minute 6797 Secretary

It was agreed that a Contract of Service for a period of Three Years be prepared for the Secretary, Mr A. S. Webb. The relevant details to be prepared by Mr T. W. Rudd and presented to the Board for confirmation.

Thursday 22nd June 1972

Minute 6801 Sinfin Sports Ground

Discussion took place regarding the damage to Sinfin and the possible erection of a fence to prevent future vandalism and it was decided that a Sub-Committee be formed to deal with this matter.

Minute 6802 The Ram

The appointment of Mr Stuart Robinson as Advertising/Circulation Manager was confirmed at a salary of £2,000 plus commission over Gross Receipts of £20,000 for Advertising and Sponsoram.

Minute 6803 New Floodlighting System

Discussion took place regarding additional costs due to the type of soil encountered during the installation of the foundations. It was agreed that this matter be left until the cost figure became available. It was reported by Mr F. W. Innes that no figure had been mentioned to him.

Minute 6804 Proposed New Stand

Mr F. W. Innes reported that meetings were proceeding with the Brewery regarding the Baseball Hotel and subsequent development.

Minute 6805 Secretary

The Chairman stated that a Contract of Service had been prepared by Mr T. W. Rudd and was now being left to the Chairman for completion.

Minute 6806 Balance at Bank

It was reported that the Club's credit balance at the Bank stood at £58,254 and on deposit £50,000 with Lombard North Central Limited and £50,000 with National Westminster Bank Finance (C.I.) Limited.

Minute 6807 Season tickets

Season ticket sales in respect of the Season 1972–73 stood at £267,924.

Minute 6809 Correspondence – Stadia Catering Limited

It was reported at the Meeting that the Division of Profits for 1971–72 Season showed an amount of £900 in excess of a guaranteed minimum of £3,000 per year.

Minute 6810 Car Parking at 97 Shaftesbury Crescent

It was reported that an application had been made for Planning Permission for this work.

HOME			**AWAY**		

League Division 1

14/08/1971	Manchester United	2–2	21/08/1971	Leicester City	2–0
18/08/1971	West Ham United	2–0	24/08/1971	Coventry City	2–2
28/09/1971	Southampton	2–2	31/08/1971	Ipswich Town	0–0
11/09/1971	Stoke City	4–0	04/09/1971	Everton	2–0
25/09/1971	West Bromwich Albion	0–0	18/09/1971	Chelsea	1–1
09/10/1971	Tottenham Hotspur	2–2	02/10/1971	Newcastle United	1–0
23/10/1971	Arsenal	2–1	16/10/1971	Manchester United	0–1
06/11/1971	Crystal Palace	3–0	30/10/1971	Nottingham Forest	2–0
20/11/1971	Sheffield United	3–0	13/11/1971	Wolverhampton Wanderers	1–2
04/12/1971	Manchester City	3–1	27/11/1971	Huddersfield Town	1–2
18/12/1971	Everton	2–0	11/12/1971	Liverpool	2–3
01/01/1972	Chelsea	1–0	27/12/1971	Leeds United	0–3
29/01/1972	Coventry City	1–0	08/01/1972	Southampton	2–1
19/02/1972	Nottingham Forest	4–0	22/01/1972	West Ham United	3–3
04/03/1972	Wolverhampton Wanderers	2–1	12/02/1972	Arsenal	0–2
18/03/1972	Leicester City	3–0	11/03/1972	Tottenham Hotspur	1–0
22/03/1972	Ipswich Town	1–0	25/03/1972	Stoke City	1–1
01/04/1972	Leeds United	2–0	28/03/1972	Crystal Palace	1–0
03/04/1972	Newcastle United	0–1	05/04/1972	West Bromwich Albion	0–0
15/04/1972	Huddersfield Town	3–0	08/04/1972	Sheffield United	4–0
01/05/1972	Liverpool	1–0	22/04/1972	Manchester City	0–2

League Cup

08/09/1971	Leeds United	0–0	27/09/1971	Leeds United	0–2

FA Cup

15/01/1972	Shrewsbury	2–0	29/02/1972	Arsenal	0–0
05/02/1972	Notts County	6–0	13/03/1972	Arsenal	0–1
26/02/1972	Arsenal	2–2			

Texaco Cup

15/09/1971	Dundee Utd	6–2		29/09/1971	Dundee Utd	2–3
20/10/1971	Stoke City	3–2		03/11/1971	Stoke City	1–1
24/11/1971	Newcastle	1–0		08/12/1971	Newcastle	3–2
26/04/1972	Airdrieonians	2–1		26/01/1972	Airdrieonians	0–0

Friendlies

07/08/1971	Schalke 04	2–0		28/07/1971	Schalke	3–1
15/11/1971	Werder Bremmen	6–2		30/07/1971	Werder Bremmen	2–1
				03/08/1971	Go Ahead Deventer	2–0
				09/08/1971	Nuneaton Borough	1–2
				26/10/1971	Swindon Town	1–1
				14/12/1971	Olympiakos	1–3

SEASON SUMMARY

Football League Division One:	Champions
FA Cup:	Fifth Round
Football League Cup:	Second Round
Texaco Cup:	Winners
Central League:	Champions
Average League Attendance:	33,161
Highest Attendance:	39,622 v. Arsenal (FA Cup)
Top League Scorers:	Hinton (15)
	O'Hare (13)
	Hector (12)

SEASON 1972–73

Thursday 6ᵗʰ July 1972

Minute 6812 Manager's Report

The Manager, Mr B. H. Clough was called into the Meeting and reported on relevant team matters. It was reported that Luton Town had increased their bid in respect of Barry Butlin to £44,000 but in view of limited cover playing wise, it was agreed to reject the offer.

Roy McFarland had signed a new two-year contract with a weekly salary of £150 plus a loyalty service bonus of £5,000 to be paid during the first three years of the Contract.

Archie Gemmill had not yet re-signed but would be meeting Manager during the course of the next few days.

It was reported that Alan Durban would this year complete 10 years' service with the Club and would be due a testimonial game.

Minute 6813 Season tickets 1972–73

It was reported that Season ticket sales in respect Season 1972–73 had now reached £283,000.

Minute 6814 Balance at Bank

It was reported that the Club's credit balance stood at £64,000. A further £100,000 being on deposit.

Minute 6815 The Ram

A lengthy discussion took place regarding various proposals for publishing *The Ram* next Season. It was decided to accept the proposition by Mr Harry Brown. It was confirmed that Mr D. Moore would be leaving the Company and settlement details were left to Mr Keeling and the Secretary to complete.

Minute 6816 Proposed New Stand

Mr F. W. Tunes submitted a lengthy report regarding meetings with Derby Corporation Planners and Mosby Haines Partnership in respect of proposed new development of the Baseball Ground. After discussion, it was agreed that the Club inform the local authority of the progressive schemes in hand for Shaftesbury Crescent and seek information on the Corporation 's immediate plans for the Area.

Editor's Comments

On 6th July a letter was sent to the Town Clerk at Derby Corporation regarding the future of the Baseball Ground. The case was made that the season's average attendance was 33,163 and the total ground capacity was 38,750 of which 14,750 were seats. 'It is the wish of the club to provide comfortable accommodation for spectators increasing the capacity of the ground to 50,000 with seating for 25,000, and also to upgrade the whole of the ground including enlarging and improving the pitch to international standard, to provide facilities in a stadium appropriate to a club of First Division status and of a quality and comfort of which the town of Derby can be proud.'

The initial proposal would be to build two new stands to replace the ABC Main Stand and the Normanton End Stand. The new main stand would provide 7,000 seats and standing space for 6,000 and the Normanton End Stand would accommodate 5,200 seats and 4,400 standing spaces, all covered.

This would entail closing Vulcan Street, purchasing the Baseball Hotel from the brewery and having many of the houses along Shaftesbury Crescent cleared in line with the local housing development plan, and the land made available to the club for the expansion.

With no forthcoming reply, the club could do nothing and a similar letter is sent again two years later.

12th July: The draws for the first round of the European competitions took place – Derby drawing the Yugoslavia champions, and also debutants in the competition, Željezničar Sarajevo. Derby were not one of the 12 seeded teams in the draw and did well to avoid Ajax, Bayern Munich, Juventus, Benfica and Celtic in the early stages.

Wednesday 19th July 1972

Minute 6818 Manager's Report

Both Mr B. H. Clough and Mr P. Taylor came into the Meeting and discussed team news in general.

It was confirmed that Archie Gemmill had signed a new one-year contract at £90 per week.

It was agreed that a sauna bath be installed and that the treatment room equipment be replaced, the total cost being in the region of £850.

It was agreed that M. Green, Dentist, be offered the position of Official Club Dentist with an honorarium of £250 per annum.

It was confirmed that Burton Albion would be paid £1,000 in respect of an outstanding agreement in the transfer of Anthony Bailey to the Club. Burton Albion having accepted the money rather than play a game.

Minute 6819 Club Doctor

Discussion took place regarding a request from Dr Worthy and Dr Eisenberg for an additional payment of £250 per annum added to the present honorarium figure of £500. After discussion it was agreed to notify the Doctors that the Club could not increase the honorarium and would for Season 1972–73 require the services of only one Doctor.

Minute 6820 Balance at Bank

The Club's credit balance on Current Account stood at £64,000 with a further £100,000 being on deposit.

Minute 6821 Season tickets 1972–73

Season ticket sales in respect of Season 1972–73 had now reached a total of £302,000.

Minute 6822 Proposed New Stand

Mr F. W. Innes confirmed that Mosby Haines Partnership would be submitting a price in respect of a new proposal for Normanton Stand. The new development would include 7,500 seats.

Minute 6823 BBC Television

The Secretary confirmed that BBC Television would cover our home game with Chelsea on Saturday 19th August 1972.

Editor's Comments

At a dinner at the Pennine Hotel (14th July) in Derby to celebrate the championship win, Clough made a speech in which he criticised Sir Alf Ramsey (England Team Manager) and also the Football Association.

The Pre-Season Tour of Holland and Germany saw the team unbeaten in which they fielded the same team for all three matches: Boulton, Webster, Robson, Durban, McFarland, Todd, McGovern, Gemmill, O'Hare, Hector, Hinton. The results of the three matches were: 1–1 v. Den Haag; 2–1 v. FC Tilburg; and 2–0 v. Schalke 04.

The tour party was led by Peter Taylor as Brian Clough wished his family to go along on the trip as well, at the Club's expense, which was refused by the Chairman as they would not be insured and a potential distraction. On Tuesday 1st August 1972 it was being widely reported that the Club and Manager were about to go their separate ways but Brian Clough commented, 'It's a complete fantasy. It would be more appropriate in Disneyland.'

The Football League fined the football club £5,000 for its part in the £200,000 failed transfer of Ian Moore during the latter part of last season, in which he was paraded on the Baseball Ground pitch prior to the match with

Wolverhampton Wanderers, but three days later had signed for Manchester United. Nottingham Forest had asked for an inquiry into the affair and Clough said, after the hearing on July 13th at the League headquarters, that, 'we have been guiltless of any improper behaviour'. The League Management Committee were satisfied that Derby had breached Regulation 52(a) and warned them about how they handled future transfer dealings.

Derby were also to appear before the Football League regarding a glass-throwing incident during the Liverpool match at the end of last season, which slashed the leg of a linesman. The disciplinary committee had various options from ground closure, fines or posting of warning notices around the stadium. Given Derby's good record of crowd behaviour one of the less serious penalties was given – the display of the warning notices. Fortunately, because of Derby's segregation policy, the incident in question was pinpointed to the visiting supporters' area and verified by the police.

Sam Longson was away on holiday, and Clough wanted him to send the Football League a telegram complaining about the Football League staff and the integrity of the League Management Committee. When Longson refused, he wrote and sent a telegram anyway, making it appear to have come from the Chairman.

These outbursts led to a letter being received from the Football Association regarding the remarks made by Clough at the Championship dinner and a similar one from the Football League about the telegram sent by Clough. These two letters were received within 24 hours of each other at the beginning of August, worrying the Board as to the conduct of their Manager and the possible consequences.

The new sauna that Clough mentioned in his Board report, that was approved, had in fact already been installed without the authorisation of the Board for its purchase.

Friday 4ᵗʰ August 1972

SPECIAL BOARD MEETING

PRESENT:

Mr S. Longson (Chairman)

Sir Robertson King, KBE

Mr S. C. Bradley

Mr T. W. Rudd

Mr F. W. Innes

Mr M. Keeling

A lengthy discussion took place in respect of a letter the Club have received from the Football League and a letter that the Chairman had received from the Football Association in respect of the Manager's conduct in recent weeks in bringing the game of football and particularly Derby County, into disrepute.

After considering the matter at great length and hearing the Manager's observations, it was resolved that the Manager be severely censored for his conduct and that he strictly observe the following conditions in future.

1. Not to make any statement through any medium of communication which may, in any way, concern either the Football Association or the Football League or any of their personnel connected therewith.
2. Not to communicate with the Football Association or the Football League. All communication on behalf of the Club to be made through the Secretary.
3. That the administration of the Club is under direct control of the Secretary and the Manager must not in any way interfere with any member of the administration staff.
4. All Staff appointments to be made by the Board of Directors and salary increases to be passed accordingly.

5 All letters for materials and goods required by the Club must be authorised by the Board of Directors and the letter signed by the Secretary.

6 Any breach of the above five conditions will render the Manager liable for dismissal.

It was agreed that the Manager be informed of the above conditions in an official letter from the Chairman.

Editor's Comments

The Secretary of the Football Association, Dennis Follows, made a rare visit to the Baseball Ground for the opening match of the season against Chelsea on 19th August, and it was suggested that it was to remind the Board of the responsibility in respect of the actions of the Manager potentially bringing the game and club into disrepute.

According to newspaper reports, Derby had pulled out of deal to sign the England Under-23 winger, David Thomas from Burnley for a fee of around £200,000 at a fairly late stage in the transfer process, with Clough saying, 'I have no interest in Thomas now whatsoever.'

At a Sports Writers' lunch, Clough continued his verbal attack on the game's authority by making various comments:

'It will be a short Munich for Sir Alf with the programme overloaded as it is'; 'You can't tell Sir Alf he is wrong, which he is, or Alan Hardaker that he has too much power, which he has'; 'If I could do one thing for football it would be to wipe out England selection committees overnight – but then I couldn't get an England job to save my life.'

The FA also ruled that an article by Clough calling for a commission to discipline Sir Alf Ramsey and picking out specific players (Peter Storey and Norman Hunter) for criticism did not bring the game into disrepute with the FA Secretary, Dennis Follows, commenting, 'I have seen the article and I wouldn't think it crossed the boundary line.'

Alan Williams, respected Midlands football reporter, wrote that there was a feeling that Peter Taylor might run the club with less friction, with

Clough believing that he should have the complete power within the club, a situation denied by many of his managerial rivals.

Wednesday 23rd August 1972

Minute 6825 Manager's Report

Both the Manager, Mr B. H. Clough and Assistant Manager, Mr P. Taylor came into the meeting and discussion took place regarding team matters.

The Manager confirmed that subject to the Board's approval a bid of £250,000 had been offered to Leicester City in respect of David Nish. After discussion, it was agreed that we confirm the offer and await Leicester's decision.

It was agreed that Roger Davies be loaned to Preston North End for a period of one month subject to Football League sanction. Details of the transfer were left to the Secretary to complete.

It was agreed that £500 be paid to Mrs Jones, the widow of the Club Scout D. Jones who died whilst attending a scouts Meeting in Derby recently.

It was agreed that a payment of £100 be forwarded Club Scout, M. Walters in respect of Alan Lewis making Football League debut.

It was agreed that the following increases be made to the following Members of the Part-time Staff:

A. Oliver to be paid £5 per week

B. Newton to be paid £5 per week

Minute 6826 Aitons Sports Ground

Mr F. W. Innes confirmed that a written offer of £28,000 had been made on behalf of the Club for Aitons Sports Ground.

Minute 6827 Season tickets 1972–73

Total sales to date for Season tickets in respect Season 1972–73 stood at £319,000.

Minute 6828 Balance at Bank

The Club's credit balance at the Bank stood at £64,000 with an additional £100,000 being on deposit.

Minute 6829 European Cup First Round First Leg

Discussion took place regarding details of the visit of the Yugoslavian Champions Sarajevo on 13th September 1972. It was agreed that the game be all-ticket and prices as follows:

'B' Stand & Ley Centre	£1.50
'A' & 'C' Stand & Ley Wings	£1.25
Osmaston & Normanton Stands	£1.00
Popular Side	50p
Osmaston/Normanton Terracing & Paddock	60p
Children	25p
OAP	15p

BBC would pay the Club £4,500 in respect of showing a recording in Great Britain and it was hoped that the game could also be sold abroad at a fixed charge.

Minute 6830 Texaco Contract

It was confirmed that Texaco had paid £14,000 in exercising the option on the Ground Advertising Contract for Season 1972–73. A further £6,000 would be paid before 1st January 1973 outside the Contract as an act of good faith from Texaco.

Minute 6831 Derby Boys

It was agreed that Derby Schoolboys be allowed to use the Baseball Ground for the following games:

Monday 25th September 1972

Monday 9th October 1972

Minute 6832 BBC Television

It was confirmed that BBC TV would cover our home game with Tottenham Hotspur on Saturday 30th September 1972.

Minute 6833 Daily Express 5-a-Side Competition

It was confirmed that the Club would be entering a team in this competition.

Minute 6834 International Youth Competition

It was confirmed that the Club would accept an invitation to represent England in an Under-20-year-olds competition in Dusseldorf next Easter.

Minute 6835 Ford Transit

It was agreed the Club purchase a Mini-Bus from T. C. Harrison for transporting the Juniors to away matches and training sessions at a net cost of £1,207-31. A 12.5% discount of £206 being allowed plus a trade in price of £260 on the Club's present van.

Editor's Comments

Clough had already indicated to Leicester City that Derby were prepared to pay a substantial fee for David Nish, without clearing any valuation with the Board in advance, which due to its size would need careful consideration.

Thursday 31st August 1972

Minute 6838 Manager's Report

The Manager, Mr B. H. Clough came into the Meeting and reported on the Club's present injury position.

Barry Butlin – Cartilage Operation

Ron Webster – Slight Strain

Colin Boulton – Thigh Strain

The Manager confirmed that Roger Davies would be called back from Preston North End. The Secretary confirmed that this was due to a special clause in the temporary transfer contract.

Details of the Kleenex Player of the Match scheme were confirmed. Kleenex Tissues would pay £10 per game to a selected player plus a payment of £250 to the Club's Player of the Year.

Minute 6839 European Cup First Round Second Leg

The Secretary outlined and confirmed the following details in respect of the Club's visit to Sarajevo.

Monday 25th September 1972   Depart Birmingham Airport 10.30 a.m.

Arrive Sarajevo 1.30 p.m.

Party to stay at The Terme Hotel for three nights.

Wednesday 27th September 1972 Kick-off v. Sarajevo 7.00 p.m.

Thursday 28th September 1972   Depart Sarajevo 9.30 a.m.

Arrive Birmingham Airport 12 noon.

It was agreed that Press and guests of Directors would be allowed to join the party at £100 per head.

Minute 6840 David John Nish

Details of the transfer of Registration of Nish from Leicester City to Derby County were confirmed as follows:

Gross Fee   £250,000

5% to Football League   £12,500

5% to Player   £12,500

Total £225,000 payable as follows:

£125,000 payable within 7 days

£50,000 payable by 1st December 1972

£50,000 payable by 1st May 1973

The Board congratulated Mr S. Longson and the Secretary for the arrangement of the very favourable terms.

Minute 6841 Aitons Sports Ground

Mr F. W. Innes reported that no confirmation or the acceptance of the Club's offer had been received from Aitons.

It was agreed that a special meeting be called to deal immediately with the matter when further information became available.

Minute 6842 Balance at Bank

The Club's Credit balance at the Bank stood at £55,000 with a further £100,000 being on deposit.

Minute 6843 Season tickets 1972–73

The Secretary reported that Season ticket sales to date in respect of Season 1972–73 had reached a total of £320,000.

Minute 6844 The Sports Council

The Secretary reported on a meeting he had along with Mr F. W. Innes and representatives of the Sports Council in respect of the Club's Redevelopment Schemes. It was reported that money was available to include other sports facilities in any stand or ground improvements the Club had in mind.

It was agreed the local authority be informed of the Club's negotiations.

Editor's Comments

David Nish became Derby's and Britain's biggest transfer when he signed from Leicester City. Nish was the youngest ever FA Cup Final captain when he led the Leicester team out in the 1969 Final against Manchester City and had been a regular player in the England Under-23 team, although he lost the Leicester captaincy during the previous season and his form since then had not been great.

Clough said, 'I've been interested in David for four years,' and, 'we could still do with two more players ... we must press on and hope for the best.' Newspapers were speculating that Derby had also bid for Leicester City goalkeeper, Peter Shilton, in a double deal and Shilton's name was one of those players Clough would like.

Nish would not be eligible to play in the European Cup matches until the quarter-final stage should Derby reach that far.

5th September: Following the weekend's victory over Liverpool, Clough launched an attack against his own supporters again, calling them 'a disgrace ... unworthy of the team' in a criticism of those not attending and those that did come along for not cheering loud enough. Sam Longson moved quickly to distance himself and the club from the comments and issued a strong statement: 'We take the opposite view about our fans. We had a reduced gate – 32,524 – because of holidays, the Olympics on television, the glorious weather ... and so on. I just do not know how Brian can insult the fans when we have taken over £300,000 in Season ticket sales. People just won't stand for it. He'll drive them away. Now I want to publicly apologise for his remarks, and tell the fans that they are appreciated.'

Thursday 14th September 1972

Minute 6846 Manager's Report

The Manager, Mr B. H. Clough reported on relevant team matters.

Nish would replace Daniel for the home game v. Birmingham City and no injuries had occurred following the European Game v. Željezničar Sarajevo.

It was confirmed that D. Nish had signed a two-year contract with a two-year option and would receive £125 per week. The signing bonus would be paid in four parts:

£3,125 by 30th June 1973

£3,125 by 30th June 1974

£3,125 by 30th June 1975

£3,125 by 30th June 1976

Minute 6847 Balance at Bank

The Club's overdrawn balance at the Bank stood at £74,000.

Minute 6848 Aitons Sports Ground

Mr F. W. lnnes confirmed that the Club's offer of £30,000 in respect of Aitons Sports Ground at Raynesway had been accepted. We are at present awaiting formal signature of Contract. The Chairman on behalf of the Board congratulated Mr T. W. Rudd for bringing the matter to his attention and to Mr F. W. lnnes for his efforts in securing the property for the Club.

Minute 6849 Independent Television

It was confirmed that ATV would cover our home game with Sheffield United on Saturday 28th October 1972.

Thursday 21st September 1972

Minute 6851 Manager's Report

The Manager, Mr B. H. Clough came into the Meeting along with Mr P. Taylor, Assistant Manager, and reported on relevant team matters.

It was confirmed that the Central League game v. West Bromwich Albion Res. has been brought forward to 21st September 1972 with a three o'clock kick-off.

It was also confirmed that Alan Durban would complete 10 years' service with the Club during July 1973 and a written request had been submitted to the Football League in respect of a Testimonial Game for this player.

Minute 6852 Balance at Bank

The Club's overdrawn balance at the Bank to date stood at £72,000 with £100,000 still being on deposit awaiting transfer.

Minute 6854 Derby Boys

The Secretary confirmed that Derby Boys would play Birmingham Boys at the Baseball Ground, kick-off 7.00 p.m. on Monday next, 25th September 1972.

Minute 6855 Football League Pension Scheme

It was confirmed that the Football League had now completed arrangements with the Trustees for the confirmation of a new Pension for employees.

The Chairman and Secretary on behalf of the Club signed the Agreement to the transfer. In so far as the Club are concerned, contributory aspects would remain as previous but greater benefits would be received by the employees.

Minute 6856 Public Liability Insurance

The Secretary outlined proposals from the Football League in respect of them taking over Group Public Liability and Employers Liability Cover through S. W. Taylor Ex Co. , Brokers Limited, London. After discussion, the Chairman proposed that the Club look carefully into this matter and before final sanction be given, the amount of financial saving to the Club be looked at. It was agreed that the Secretary make the necessary enquiries.

Minute 6857 National Westminster Bank Limited

Confirmation was received from the National Westminster Bank in respect of the Club's borrowing powers for Season 1972–73 and that the following would apply.

An overdraft limit of £50,000 plus a temporary and occasional excess of £30,000 coupled with an agreement in principle to extend the facilities by a further £20,000 subject to the provision of additional Guarantees.

It was confirmed that there would be no change to the previous year's borrowing.

Minute 6858 Mr Peter Taylor – Loan

It is agreed to loan Mr Peter Taylor, Assistant Manager, £5,000 at an interest to be repaid at 5% and repayments to be £100 per month taken out of his wages.

Minute 6859 European Bonuses – Manager and Assistant Manager

It was agreed that the following bonuses be paid to the Manager and Assistant Manager in respect of the European Cup for Season 1972–73.

£500 each for the Club playing in the Second Round

£1,000 each for the Club playing in the Third Round

£1,500 each for the Club playing in the Fourth Round

£3,000 each for the Club playing in the Semi-final

£5,000 each for the Club playing in the Final

Minute 6860 Weekly Financial Breakdown

The Secretary submitted the following financial breakdown of the running cost of the Company on approximation of a week to week basis.

The figures did not include any percentage for Season ticket takings.

Weekly Financial Breakdown

Receipts		Payments	
1st Team v. Birmingham (H)	6,492	Wages: Players & Staff	4,150
v. WBA (A)	1,288	Hotel	125
2nd Team v. Burnley (H)	71	Coach	25
Adverts & TV Fees & Programmes	500	Overheads	2,200
Approx. deficit for fortnight	1,500		
Birmingham	2,718		
F.L. %	222		
Petty Cash	**420**		
	9,860		
	9,860		

NB. Derby County Promotions transfer to the Club account approximately £1,000 per week.

Editor's Comments

There was growing speculation in the national press regarding the Manager's position as after three months he had still not signed a contract, believed to be worth £80,000 over a five-year period. Following the letter sent by the Directors in the summer, Clough saw it as a 'gagging order' to restrain his outspoken comments that were causing some embarrassment to the Club. Dave Mackay's name had been mentioned as a possible successor if the contract deadline was not met, and Aston Villa would be interested in Clough and Taylor's services, should they become available.

25th September: Colin Todd (along with Chelsea's Alan Hudson) was banned from international football, on the recommendation of the Under-23 committee, for a period of two years, for not travelling on an England tour of Eastern Europe, which most pundits regarded with some criticism. Todd was exhausted after the long, hard season and had told Sir Alf Ramsey personally four times and written a letter with his explanation. *The Sun* commented, 'You have to be some kind of nut to believe we are so well stocked with class players that we can afford to sideline two of them. The decision inevitably mauls our chances of success at Munich in the 1974 World Cup.' Clough agreed: 'it is staggering ... incredible. Whoever is in charge and responsible for the decision, has made the wrong one. Half the world and most of Europe will be laughing their heads off.'

25th September: The Derby County party of players and Directors flew out to Sarajevo from Birmingham airport, returning on the Thursday morning.

27th September: The away leg of the European Cup tie against Željezničar Sarajevo was scheduled to be televised by ITV, but at the last moment Željezničar refused permission for the transmission , denying the Derby fans the sight of their team playing away in Europe for the first time. ITV had negotiated a contract with the Yugoslav national television organisation and commentator Hugh Johns and a production crew had flown out with the team. In the end ITV switched their coverage to the Leeds United v. MKE Ankaragucu game, and Hugh Johns, having travelled all that way, commented that it 'left me angry and speechless'.

2nd October: The draw for the second round of the European Cup took place in Rome.

Wednesday 4th October 1972

Minute 6861 Manager's Report

Mr Peter Taylor, Assistant Manager, came into the Meeting and delivered a report on relevant team matters and announced a probable team to play Chelsea that evening.

It was agreed that the following bonuses be paid to the Training Staff in respect of winning the First Round of the European Cup in Sarajevo.

J. Gordon – £50

J. Sheridan – £25

G. Guthrie – £25

It was agreed that a bonus of £250 each be paid to the Manager and Assistant Manager for reaching the Third Round of the Football League Cup.

After discussion, it was agreed that Roger Davies would be fined one week's wages in respect of him being sent off the field in the recent Reserves match at Stoke City.

Minute 6862 Balance at Bank

The Club's credit balance at the Bank to date stood at £22,000.

Minute 6863 European Cup – Second Round

The Secretary confirmed that a Directive from UEFA had been received in respect of no drinks being allowed to be served on the night of the Benfica game. It was agreed that we would have to comply with these Rules but that the Secretary would write to the Football Association and express our views on the matter.

Prices for the game were confirmed and it was agreed that there would be no increase from the last European game and that seats would be priced £1.50, £1.25, £1 and ground and terracing at 60p and 50p.

The Secretary outlined details of arrangements for the week commencing the 23rd when the Benfica Party will be arriving in Derby. It was confirmed that there would be a Civic Reception at the Council House on the Tuesday evening, the 24th, for Directors, Management and their wives and Officials from Benfica and that a Pre-match Banquet/Reception would be held at the La Gondola Restaurant at 4.00 p.m. on the day of the match. The usual Directors and Football Officials will be invited.

For the trip to Lisbon, it was confirmed that a BEA Air Tours Charter Flight had been booked and would depart East Midlands Airport on Monday 6th November, returning to East Midlands on Thursday 9th. It was agreed that guests would be invited and charged £100 but would stay at a separate Hotel away from the Team.

It was agreed that the Secretary contact Texaco with a view to them paying a further £2,000 in respect of Ground Advertising for this match taking into consideration that the game would be shown on BBC Television throughout England and also it is hoped, throughout the Continent. The matter was left to the Secretary and Mr Keeling to pursue.

EUROPEAN CUP FIRST ROUND FINANCIAL BREAKDOWN

GROSS RECEIPTS		EXPENSES	
Gate	18,490.35	Referee & Linesmen	275.15
TV Fees	4,500.00	Checkers	290.00
Sponsoram	1,000.00	Advertising	200.00
		Police	500.00
		Refreshments	100.00
		Floodlights	20.00

	Presents	200.00
	UEFA 3%	554.71
	UEFA TV 10%	450.00
	Away Game	
	Hotel Sarajevo	1,000.00
	Aircraft	4,000.00
	Profit (approx.)	16,000.00
23,990.35		23,990.35

Profit approx.	£15,490	
Deduct Bonuses for entry into Europe		
Manager	£1,500	
Assistant Manager	£1,500	
Players 14 x £500 =	£7,000	£10090
First Round Net Profit	£6,400	

Editor's Comments

16th October: Press reports suggested that Stoke City were preparing a £100,000 transfer offer for Terry Hennessey, with the Stoke Manager, Tony Waddington, saying, 'We have an interest in Hennessey – provided Derby say he is available' and had him watched in the last couple of games. Stoke's alternate target was Mike Doyle of Manchester City, who they ultimately signed as Hennessey was not available for transfer.

24th October: A Civic Reception was held at the Council House for the Benfica and Derby Directors, UEFA Delegates and other invited guests, whilst the Benfica team would be staying at the Pennine Hotel. Prior to the game there would be a pre-match meal at La Gondola. Due to the interest in the tie, an additional press box had to be created, situated behind the dugouts and equipped with phones for international calls.

It was announced by the Government that VAT (a replacement for the SET and Purchase Tax) was to be introduced onto the cost of a match ticket from 1st April 1973, which was likely to cost Derby an additional £50,000 against a backdrop of falling attendances. Ultimately, this would be passed to the fans and push up the cost of match tickets. At the same time, all transfer fees were also going to be liable for 10% tax with clubs claiming this was reintroducing the old Entertainment Tax that was removed in 1960.

Thursday 26th October 1972

Minute 6866 Manager's Report
Mr B. H. Clough, the Manager, came into the Meeting and reported on relevant team matters over the past fortnight.

The Chairman on behalf of the Board, congratulated the Manager and Players on their success in the European Cup Second Round v. Benfica in gaining a 3–0 home victory.

Minute 6867 ATV Television
It was confirmed that the home match v. Arsenal on 25th November would be televised by ATV.

Minute 6868 Anglo–Italian Competition
It was reported that an invitation for the Club to enter the Anglo–Italian Competition in the summer of 1973 had been refused.

Minute 6869 Mayoral Reception
An invitation from the Mayor and Representatives of the Council had been received to attend an Informal Luncheon Party prior to our home game with Arsenal on 25th November.

It was agreed that the Chairman and three other representatives of the Club would attend. Final details would be confirmed at the next Meeting.

Minute 6870 Ian Buxton Testimonial

It was confirmed that a Derby County XI would play a Luton Town XI on Monday 27th November with a kick-off of 7.15 p.m. in respect of the Ian Buxton Testimonial Fund.

The Secretary confirmed that Football League permission had been granted.

Minute 6871 UEFA & Drinks at Football Grounds

The Secretary reported on correspondence with the Football Association and UEFA and confirmed that the Club would be allowed to serve drinks at the Ground at all future European Games providing that the high standard of spectator control was maintained. It was also confirmed that should any incidents occur, the Club would be held fully responsible for the supporters' actions and a serious penalty would be imposed on the Club.

Minute 6872 Balance at Bank

The credit balance on the Club's current account stood at £33,000 to date with a credit balance on the Promotions Account of £3,500.

Minute 6873 Aitons Sports Ground

Mr T. W. Rudd confirmed that the Contract was to hand in respect of the Club purchasing Aitons Sports Ground on a ninety-nine-year lease, expiry date being the year 2072. The total purchase price was £30,000, the Club having paid a deposit of £3,000.

It was agreed that a Sub-Committee be formed from within the Board in respect of discussions regarding the Sports Ground facilities.

Minute 6874 Proposed New Stand

Mr F. W. Innes confirmed that a Meeting with the Architect, Mr Haines of Mosby Haines Partnership would take place at the Ground on 1st November 1972. It was agreed that the Chairman and other Members of the Board wishing to attend be present at the Ground at 11.00 a.m.

Minute 6875 Annual General Meeting

The Draft Accounts were presented to the Board in respect of the year ending 31st July 1972 and after general discussion, it was agreed to fix the Annual General Meeting for 6th December at 10.30 a.m. in the Clubroom at the Baseball Ground.

Minute 6876 The Ram

The Secretary reported that on the first seven issues of *The Ram*, a total gross profit for the period resulted in £4,075. Total advertising for these first seven issues amounted to £2,000.

Editor's Comments

27th October: Brian Clough was ready to sign the five-year contract offered to him at the end of the previous season, with the relevant clauses removed that restricted what he could say without the Board reviewing it first, 'all they have to do now is put a contract before me and I will sign'. A day later, in front of the ITV cameras, a couple of hours before the Sheffield United match, and watched over by Sam Longson and Stuart Webb, the Manager and Assistant both signed their contracts.

Derby made their debut in the National Five-a-Side championship at the Empire Pool, Wembley on 15th November. The three-hour-long tournament contained 16 teams, 14 from the First Division and Aberdeen and Celtic from Scotland. The evening's highlights were broadcast on the BBC's *Sportsnight* programme. Amongst Derby's squad were Todd, McGovern, Hector and O'Hare and they beat QPR (2–0) and Manchester United (1–0) before losing to a late goal in a 2–3 defeat to Tottenham Hotspur, the competition winners.

As a result of a joint Derby and Liverpool representation, the FA lifted their ban on the sale of alcohol for European club competitions. UEFA had no objections, but reminded everyone that there would consequences should any ground disturbances occur as a result. The limit on alcohol sales was only ever a UEFA recommendation, but fully implemented by the FA. The reversal of that decision was welcomed by Stuart Webb.

Thursday 23rd November 1972

Minute 6878 Manager's Report

The Manager, Mr B. H. Clough came into the Meeting and reported on relevant team matters and the Club's injury position over the past few weeks.

It was confirmed that Stephen Powell had now signed Full-time Professional on a two-year Contract with a two-year option. Terms were as follows:

£45 per week

£20 per week appearance money when in First Team

£1,500 spread over a period of four years (£375 per instalment)

It was confirmed that Roy McFarland had been fined £150 by the Club in respect of his disciplinary suspension from the Football Association received due to accumulating 12 penalty points.

European Bonuses

It was confirmed that the following bonuses would be paid in respect of the Second Round European Cup tie v. Benfica.

J. Gordon £100

G. Guthrie £50

J. Sheridan £50

Minute 6879 Balance at Bank

It was confirmed that the Club's Credit balance to date stood at £3,500 with £2,500 being at present on the Promotions Account.

The Secretary confirmed that £50,000 would be due to Leicester City on 1ˢᵗ December together with £27,000 to Aitons on 8ᵗʰ December.

Minute 6882 Aitons Sports Ground

Mr T. W. Rudd confirmed that the completion date for Aitons Sports Ground would be 7ᵗʰ December. It was also confirmed that the Chairman would officially release it to the Press at the Annual General Meeting the following day.

Discussion took place regarding the current Staff employed at Raynesway and the possibility of redundancy pay should the Club dispose of their services. It was left to Mr Rudd and the Secretary to finalise details with Aitons direct and it was also confirmed that a Sub-Committee Meeting of Directors would be held on Tuesday 28ᵗʰ November at 10.30 a.m. to discuss along with the Managers the possible ancillary activities that could be incorporated within the Raynesway Sports Centre.

Minute 6883 Vice-Chairman

It was proposed by Mr S. Longson, Chairman, and unanimously agreed that Mr S. C. Bradley be appointed Vice-Chairman of the Company.

Minute 6884 Personal Accident Insurance

The Secretary confirmed that a remittance of £227.50 had been received from the Football League in respect of Barry Butlin's recent incapacity.

Minute 6885 BBC Television

It was confirmed that BBC Television would televise the Coventry City match on 9ᵗʰ December 1972. It was also confirmed that the second half of our match on 26ᵗʰ December v. Manchester United would be the subject of the sound broadcast.

Editor's Comments

The Football League had called a meeting for January to discuss the financial issues that were arising in football and inevitably would look at the reasons why attendances were falling at an alarming rate across the country.

Stuart Webb suggested that Derby were under-pricing their tickets for the European matches, but were fearful of being called greedy by their own fans. He used the Benfica game as an example, where the home attendance generated record receipts of £30,000 on a 40,000 gate; Benfica generated £175,000 for a 70,000 attendance. The reason for this was that, in common with other European clubs, their ticket prices were substantially higher (£3, £2 and £1 compared to Derby's top price ticket at £1.50) and indeed English clubs' prices were also in the same bracket. The difference in generated income could make a huge difference in the calibre of player Derby could sign.

Thursday 30th November 1972

Minute 6887 Manager's Report

The Manager, Mr B. H. Clough, came into the Meeting and reported on relevant team matters and announced a probable team to play Wolverhampton Wanderers on the coming Saturday.

It was confirmed that Roy McFarland had been suspended for two games and that during his FA suspension, his two weeks' wages would be paid by the Club.
It was confirmed that Barry Butlin had been transferred to Luton Town for a Gross Fee of £55,000. The Nett Fee payable to Derby County would be as follows:

£15,000 down

£10,000 by 1st January 1973

£10,000 by 1st February 1973

£10,000 by 1st March 1973

£5,000 by 1st April 1973

It was confirmed that due to the transfer of Butlin to Luton, it was now essential that John Sims be registered with the Football League. The Secretary confirmed that the registration would be done immediately and the £250 forwarded to the League with the balance of £250 spread over Sims' Contract.

It was confirmed that the Manager mislaid a coat of an employee whilst attending the game at Luton Town and it was agreed that the coat be replaced from Mr Bradley and the Secretary was instructed to make the necessary claim on the Club's Insurance.

Minute 6888 Balance at Bank

The credit balance on the Club's account to date stood at £4,500 with the Promotions Account in credit of £3,000.

Minute 6889 Annual General Meeting

The Annual General Meeting was confirmed for 8th December 1972. The Secretary confirmed that no nominations for the Directorship had been received to date. The Chairman also confirmed that following the Annual General Meeting, he would entertain the Board of Directors, Senior Members of the Staff and the Club's Accountant, Solicitor and Bank Manager to a Luncheon at the Coppice Hotel, Derby.

Minute 6891 Aitons Sports Ground

Discussion took place regarding the Groundsman and Steward employed by Aitons & Co. who work at the Sports Ground.

After discussions, it was agreed that the Club inform Aitons that their employment be terminated as on completion date and that Derby County Football Club would re-engage them the following day. This move would then relieve the Club of any Redundancy pay liability. It was confirmed that Mr F. W. Innes in liaison with the Manager would visit the Sports Ground during the course of the next week or so to look at Training facilities, Dressing rooms, etc.

Minute 6892 B. H. Clough – Company Car

Discussion took place regarding the Club purchasing a Company Car for the Manager. After general discussion, it was agreed that the matter be again discussed at a later date.

Minute 6893 Proposed New Stand

Mr F. W. Innes submitted a report to the Directors of various meetings held with Mr W. J. Haines of Mosby Haines Partnership and his further discussions with representatives of Bass Worthington, and the Town Clerk. It was hoped that the Report could be studied in detail and then a policy decision would be taken early in the New Year.

It was also reported that two further houses in Shaftesbury Crescent could be bought for £600 and the matter was left to Mr Innes to look into and report back at an early date.

Minute 6894 Derby Corporation

Discussion took place regarding the recent meeting and Dinner at the Council House between members of the Board and Senior Members of the Corporation and Town Council.

It was agreed that no change be made in respect of their allocation of Seasonal Box tickets to the civic dignitaries.

Two Directors' Box Tickets would be issued to the Mayor as usual and should any visiting mayors, senior officials or senior council members require tickets, they would apply in the normal way to the Secretary.

Editor's Comments

It was announced that Director Mr Fred Walters had died at his Littleover home on 1st December. He had been a Director for 22 years.

Friday 8th December 1972

ANNUAL GENERAL MEETING

PRESENT: Mr S. Longson (Chairman)

Sir Robertson King, KBE

Mr S. C. Bradley

Mr T. W. Rudd

Mr F. W. Innes

Mr M. Keeling

As a mark of respect to Director, Mr F. B. Walters who passed away on 30th November 1972 the Chairman asked the Meeting to stand in silence for one minute.

38 Shareholders attended + 2 Proxy Holders

IN ATTENDANCE: Mr A. S.Webb – Secretary

Mr W. E. Mason – Auditor

Notice Convening the Meeting

The Secretary read the Notice convening the Meeting.

Minutes of the Last Ordinary General Meeting

The Minutes of the last Ordinary General Meeting held on Friday 19th November 1971 were read, approved and signed.

Auditor's Report

The Auditors read their report to the Shareholders assembled at the Meeting.

Directors' Report & Accounts

The Chairman proposed:

'That the Directors' Report, the Revenue Account for the year ended 31st July 1972 and the Balance Sheet at that date, be and hereby be approved and adopted.'

Mr C. Cott seconded the proposition, and after dealing with general questions on the Accounts, the Chairman put the resolution to the Meeting, and declared it carried.

Election of Directors

Special Notice having been received in accordance with the provisions of Section 142 & 185 (5) of the Companies Act 1948.

Mr S. C. Bradley proposed:

'That Sir Robertson King, KBE having attained the age of 70 years, be, and is hereby re-elected an Ordinary Director of the Company.'

Mr C. Cadman seconded the resolution, which was put to the Meeting and was declared carried.

Mr T. W. Rudd proposed:

'That S. Longson having attained the age of 70 years, be, and is hereby re-elected an Ordinary Director of the Company.'

Mr A. Pinder seconded the resolution, which was put to the Meeting and carried.

Mr M. Keeling proposed:

'That Sir Robertson King, KBE, President retiring under Paragraph 77(a) of the Company's Articles of Association, be, and is hereby re-elected President of the Company.'

Mr A. Atkins seconded the resolution, which was put to the Meeting and carried.

Mr F. W. Innes proposed:

'That Mr S. Longson, Vice-President retiring under Paragraph 77(b) of the Company's Articles of Association, be, and is hereby re-elected Vice-President of the Company.'

Mr S. Gould seconded the resolution, which was put to the Meeting and carried.

Mr S. C. Bradley proposed:

'That Mr M. Keeling, Director retiring under Paragraph 77(c) of the Company's Articles of Association, be, and is hereby re-elected a Director of the Company.'

Mr R. Joell seconded the proposition, which was put to the Meeting and carried.

General

The Chairman, Mr S. Longson, paid tribute to his fellow Directors, Management and Players for their contribution towards the efficient running of the Club.

The Manager, Mr B. H. Clough addressed the Meeting on general team matters and the Meeting closed with a vote of thanks to the Chairman and Board proposed by Mr B. Webb and seconded by Mr L. Overton, Shareholders in the Company.

Editor's Comments

The year-end accounts published at the Annual General Meeting showed the Club managed a healthy £80,000 profit despite the following:

- Expenditure in the playing staff
- Major ground changes and upgrade in facilities
- Installation of the very latest floodlights
- A doubling of the wage bill from the previous season
- And boosted by the activities of the Derby County Promotions organisation.

The Meeting itself was concluded in less than 45 minutes with the approval of the shareholders. The Manager mentioned that there were differences of opinion between the Board and himself in the period before signing his new contract, but these were now behind them.

Thursday 14ᵗʰ December 1972

Before the ordinary business of the Meeting commenced, the Chairman, Mr S. Longson paid tribute to the services rendered to the Board of Directors by the late Mr F. B. Walters who had served the Club for many years as Director, Vice-President and Chairman.

Minute 6896 Manager's Report

The Manager, Mr B. H. Clough came into the Meeting and reported on relevant team matters over the past fortnight.

It was confirmed that Brighton & Hove Albion had made a written bid for the transfer of registration of Archie Gemmill for a sum of £75,000. It was agreed that this sum was totally inadequate and the Secretary was informed to notify Brighton that a fee for this Player would be at least £150,000.

Minute 6897 Sinfin Training Ground

Mr T. W. Rudd confirmed that planning application had been submitted to the Town Council in respect of Sinfin Lane Sports Ground and the application would be considered at the Council Meeting on 16th January 1973.

Minute 6898 Balance at Bank

The Club's overdrawn balance at the Bank to date stood at £70,000 and the Promotion Account to date stood at £3,000.

Minute 6899 BBC Television

It was confirmed that BBC Television would cover our match with Norwich City on *Match Of The Day* on 6th January 1973.

Minute 6900 Texaco

The Secretary outlined discussions with Texaco in respect of advertising for Season 1972–73 and confirmed the following:

Texaco would pay Derby County Football Club £14,000 by 1st September 1972, £6,000 by 1st January 1973 and a further £2,000 in respect of each European Cup home game.

Minute 6901 Bass Worthington

The Secretary confirmed that the Advertising Contract with Bass Worthington in respect of two sites on the Shaftesbury Crescent Side of the Ground were up for renewal on 1st January 1973. The present Contract included an Option Clause and it is suggested that the Chairman and Secretary meet Members of the Brewery for discussions on the matter early in the New Year.

Minute 6902 Derby Corporation Transport Department

A letter was received from the General Manager, Derby Corporation Passenger Transport, in respect of them supplying the Club with a luxury coach built to our own requirements and for the exclusive use of Derby County Football Club. In return the Corporation would require a minimum guarantee of a four-year Contract and a rate per mile of 28p. After general discussion, it was agreed that the matter be left on the table for further discussion.

Tuesday 2ⁿᵈ January 1973

Minute 6904 Manager's Report

The Manager, Mr B. H. Clough, came into the Meeting and reported on relevant team matters.

It was reported that Ron Webster, who had accumulated 12 penalty points under the FA Disciplinary System, would be suspended for the following two First Team games.

Norwich City – Football League

Peterborough United – FA Cup

David Nish has now recovered from injury and would be available for selection.

It was confirmed that the Manager and Mr Innes would visit Raynesway Sports Ground and inspect the existing facilities and report back to the next Board Meeting as to the immediate requirements of the Club.

It was confirmed that Stoke City had not confirmed a suitable date for the proposed rearranged Easter game. It was left to the Secretary to contact Stoke again and report back at the next Meeting.

Minute 6905 B. H. Clough – Company Car

It was confirmed that the Club would purchase the Manager's existing car from him at a fee of £3,200. The Club would be responsible for Insurance and Road Fund Licence.

Minute 6906 Balance at Bank

The overdrawn balance at the Bank to date stood at £80,000. The Secretary reported that a further £5,000 had been transferred from the Promotions Account that particular day. Total donations received from Promotions up to 1st January 1973 amounted to £30,000.

The Westminster Bank confirmed that our present overdraft borrowing rate was still 2% over base rate with a minimum of 6%. Base rate at present time standing at 7.5%, thus overdraft rate currently 9.5%.

Minute 6907 Football League Meeting

The Secretary reported on the recent Secretaries Meeting at the Great Western Hotel when the commercial side of football together with implications of VAT were discussed. In broad terms the Football League require the whole 92 Clubs to be involved with them in the marketing of Club badges which would be issued throughout abroad. It was envisaged that the Scheme would not interfere with participating Clubs' present activities as the proposals were on a National level and not at a local level.

It was reported that the Football League were issuing an official League Train which would be available to Clubs on hire during the course of the year.

Minute 6908 Football League, Chairmen's Meeting 16.1.73

The Chairman laid down proposals which had been forwarded by the Management Committee of the Football League for discussions at the Chairmen's Meeting. A general discussion took place and various views were expressed and it was agreed that the Chairman and Secretary represent the Club at this meeting and report back on any relevant matters discussed.

Minute 6909 Sinfin Lane Sports Ground

A letter from Evans Limited of Leeds was read out in respect of their interest in purchasing Sinfin Lane Sports Ground for development.

Mr F. W. Innes confirmed that planning permission had been applied for and the matter would be considered at the Derby Corporation's next meeting.

EUROPEAN CUP DRAW, FRANKFURT – 17th January 1973

The Chairman confirmed that the Secretary, Mr Taylor and possibly Mr Keeling would attend and represent the Club at the European Cup draw in Frankfurt on 17th January 1973.

Minute 6910 John Robson – Aston Villa

The transfer of registration of John Robson to Aston Villa Football Club was confirmed.

A Gross Fee of £94,445

5% to Football League £4,722

5% to Player £4,722

Leaving Net Fee payable to Derby County £85,000

The Fee of £85,000 to be paid as follows:

£28,000 on within 7 days

£29,000 by 1st May 1973

£28,000 by 1st December 1973

Minute 6911 Testing of Crush Barriers

The Secretary read a letter from the Football Association indicating that they where offered a free service of the testing of crush barriers in order that the standards of Grounds be brought up to the Wheatley Report. It was agreed that the Club would take advantage of this offer.

Minute 6912 Manchester United, Boxing Day – Police Enquiry

The Secretary reported that Derby Police had called in an independent Chief Constable from Nottingham to look into the crowd problems outside the Ground prior to the game with Manchester United.

The Secretary confirmed that statements had been given from most members of the administration and checking staff and the Club where awaiting the Report of the enquiry.

Minute 6913 F. B. Walters

A letter was read from Mrs F. B. Walters thanking the Board for their kindness and messages of sympathy during the death of her husband.

Minute 6914 Staff Bonuses

It was agreed that the following Staff bonuses be paid to the Administration Staff in respect or additional work following the winning of the League Championship and the involvement in European Competition 1972–73 Season.

Secretary £350

Assistant Secretary £100

and the sum of £100 to be distributed amongst the other administration staff at the discretion of the Secretary.

Editor's Comments

Another offer for John Robson had been received by Birmingham City for £120,000 but this offer was dealt with by Mr Notley, Clough's personal assistant, instead of following the established procedure of going via the Secretary and then the Board, with a recommendation from the Manager. By not doing so, the Club lost £25,000. Robson had come from a non-League background and had been virtually ever-present during his time at the Club since making his debut in March 1968. He was also awarded seven England Under-23 caps. In total he made 213 starts, one substitute appearance and scored five goals. With the signing of David Nish, his first team opportunities were going to be limited and with the likes of Alan Lewis and Peter Daniel also in the Reserves, the club were prepared to let him go to Aston Villa for a reasonable fee.

Thursday 11ᵗʰ January 1973

Minute 6916 Manager's Report

The Manager, Mr B. H. Clough came into the Meeting and reported on the Club's present injury position. He reported that Alan Hinton had a groin strain but was expected to be fit for the forthcoming Cup tie with Peterborough United on Saturday.

It was confirmed that the Central League game v. Wolverhampton Wanderers Reserves had been arranged for Friday evening, 12ᵗʰ January 1973 with an evening kick-off of 7.30 p.m.

Minute 6917 Balance at Bank

The Club's overdrawn balance at the Bank to date stood at £55,000 with a £4,000 credit balance on the Promotions Account.

Minute 6918 Derby County's Sports Ground – Raynesway

Mr F. W. Innes confirmed that after discussions with the Manager and Trainer, it was now clear what requirements where needed for Raynesway to be converted into a modern training ground for everyday use by the Team.

It was confirmed that Mr Perks of F. Perks & Co. would be consulted on the matter of additional buildings.

Minute 6919 Vice-Presidency

The Chairman, Mr Longson confirmed the Club's general policy in filling vacancies from within the Board of Directors whenever a vacancy occurred with a Vice-Presidency.

It was therefore proposed by Mr T. W. Rudd and seconded by Mr F. W. Innes that Mr S. C. Bradley be officially appointed Vice-President of the Club caused by the death of Mr F. B. Walters.

This proposition was unanimously accepted by the Board and Mr Bradley thanked the Members for their confidence.

Minute 6920 Any Other Business

The Chairman outlined discussions he had had with the Groundsman in respect of wages and after general discussion it was agreed that the Chairman look into the general wage structure of the Ground Staff and report back to the Board.

The Chairman also raised the point of the amount of wine, beer and spirits being consumed on the Premises and it was agreed that the Secretary prepare some form of monthly return in order that the Board could have a more clear picture in this direction.

Editor's Comments

On 17th January, the Secretary and Directors Bill Rudd and Bob Innes headed to the German Football Association offices in Frankfurt for the quarter-final draw of the European Cup. This saw Derby come up against Czechoslovakian champions, Spartak Trnava, who were rank outsiders, although Clough calmed everyone by saying, 'There can be no weak side left in such a competition as this, not at this stage.'

Thursday 25th January 1973

Minute 6922 Manager's Report

The Manager, Mr B. H. Clough came into the meeting and reported on relevant team matters over the last fortnight.

It was confirmed that Stephen Powell had now totalled 12 disciplinary points under the FA Ruling and would be suspended for two games commencing 30th January 1973 and would miss the FA Cup game with Tottenham Hotspur and the League game with Birmingham City.

It was confirmed that the Scottish FA had asked about the availability or John McGovern (Under-23) and John O'Hare in respect of the forthcoming representative games due to take place in Scotland in February. It was agreed that the Scottish FA be notified that if selected, these players would be available.

It was confirmed that Andrew Rowlands, at present an amateur with the Club would be signing full-time professional in the near future.

It was reported that Tony Parry was in some financial difficulty in respect of his mortgage repayments and it was agreed that the Club would help him in this matter and it was left to the Secretary to liaise with Mr Rudd and make the necessary arrangements for a further loan and subsequent repayment.

Minute 6923 Raynesway Sports Ground

Mr F. W. Innes confirmed that he had visited Raynesway with the Manager, Jimmy Gordon and Mr Perks and the Club were awaiting proposed detailed drawings of Dressing Room accommodation that where being prepared by Mr Perks.

Minute 6924 Balance at Bank

The Club's balance at the bank to date stood at £58,000 overdrawn with a £3,000 credit balance on the Promotions Account.

Minute 6925 European Cup Quarter Final v. Spartak Trnava

Discussion took place regarding proposed prices for the forthcoming quarter-final European Cup game at the Baseball Ground and after due consideration it was proposed by Mr T. W. Rudd and seconded by Mr S. C. Bradley that:

"B" & Ley Stand Centre	£1.75
"A", "C" and Ley Wings	£1.50
Osmaston & Normanton	£1.25
Paddock, Osmaston & Normanton Terracing	70p
Popular Side Terracing	60p

The Secretary reported that a capacity gate of 36,000 would bring in a total gross gate of approximately £33,500.

It was also confirmed that Independent Television would be covering the game and a fee of £6,000 had been offered to the Club. This together with suggested fees for overseas sales, the Fee ranging from £500 to £750 per Country.

Minute 6926 Bass Worthington

The Chairman gave details of recent discussions with the Advertising People of Bass Worthington in respect of the Brewery advertising boards at the Baseball Ground.

The Club had fixed the price of £2,000 per board per annum.

This amount would have to receive Central Office confirmation and the Brewery had requested time for this request to be considered.

Minute 6927 Football League Chairmen's Meeting – 16th January 1973

The Chairman confirmed the Secretary's Report as forwarded to the Directors on the recent Football League Chairmen's Meeting. He did, however, raise points on various items which had caused heavy discussion.

Minute 6928 Central League

The Secretary confirmed the Bury Reserve Central League game scheduled to be played at the Baseball Ground on Saturday 3rd February 1973 would now be played on Wednesday 7th February 1973 with an afternoon Kick-off of 3.00 p.m.

Minute 6929 ATV – FA Cup Tie

It was confirmed that ATV would be televising the forthcoming FA Cup tie with Tottenham Hotspur and the fee to be received would be £250.

Minute 6930 Sinfin Lane Sports Ground

Mr F. W. lnnes reported that the Application for Sinfin Lane had been refused and that on behalf of the Club he would be making a formal appeal.

Further to our second application in respect or buildings and warehousing this, we were informed by the Corporation, would be advertised in the local press in respect of any objections to our scheme and the application would be raised at the Council's next meeting.

Minute 6931 Police Report – Boxing Day v. Manchester United

The Chairman reported on the satisfactory conclusion of the Police Report and the Meeting between the Secretary and himself together with the Chief Constable and Senior Officers at Butterley Hall.

It was agreed that a video tape and extra tannoy systems outside the Ground would be installed to improve general liaison with the Police and Club Officials. It was left with the Secretary to arrange.

Editor's Comments

The crowd incidents discussed regarding the Manchester United fixture were investigated, and it was found that many fans arrived late (being a Bank Holiday, usual public transport services were not running) at the ground, and this also coincided with the late arrival of two special trains carrying 1,000 Manchester United fans. This, one way or another, led to a large mass of people in Vulcan Street trying to gain entrance to the Popside and Ley Stand. This caused temporary closure of some of the gates whilst queues could be processed and pressure relieved.

Friday 9th February 1973

Minute 6933 Manager's Report

The Manager, Mr B. H. Clough came into the Meeting and reported on the Club's injury position and the probable Team to play away at Birmingham on Saturday. With the current list of injuries, it was expected that Parry and Sims would both play in the First Team.

It was agreed that an increase of £4 per week be paid to John Sheridan as from 1st February 1973 and that his bonus be up-lifted from half first team bonus to full first team bonus per week.

It was confirmed that Ricky Marlowe had been temporarily transferred for a period of two months to Limerick Football Club. The Player would return to the Baseball Ground on 1st April 1973.

It was agreed that the Club should loan Jeff Bourne the sum of £325 in respect of a house loan and the Secretary would seek the necessary confirmation from the Football League.

It was reported that Everton Football Club had turned down a written request for £100,000 clear for Henry Newton and it was agreed that this matter be allowed to lie on the table for the present time.

The Chairman on behalf of the Members of the Board, congratulated the Management and Players on their tremendous success over Tottenham Hotspur in the replay at White Hart Lane on Wednesday 7th February when they defeated Tottenham Hotspur 5 goals to 3.

Minute 6934 Midland Intermediate League

The Secretary confirmed that the dates for the Final tie in the Midland Intermediate League Challenge Cup Final v. Stoke City would be as follows:

At Stoke on Wednesday 25th April 1973

At Derby on Wednesday 2nd May 1973

Minute 6935 Ground Staff Wages

The Chairman confirmed the following wage increases in respect of the Groundstaff as from 1st February 1973.

R. Smith – £36 per week, no overtime to be paid

B. Hill – £23 per week, overtime to be paid

Minute 6936 Balance at Bank

The overdrawn balance at the Bank to date stood at £46,300 and the credit balance on Promotions at £500.

Minute 6937 Television Coverage v. Queen's Park Rangers

It was agreed that the Club would allow the BBC in conjunction with the Football Association to televise the highlights of our Fifth Round Cup game on Saturday 24th February v. Queen's Park Rangers. The fee to Derby County would be £250.

Minute 6939 Tony Parry Loan

It was confirmed by the Secretary that following a Meeting with Mr Rudd, it was agreed that confirmation had been received from the Football League to loan Parry an additional loan (£305.35).

The Secretary was undertaking to ensure that the necessary standing orders were completed in order that Parry would not get into any more financial difficulty.

The Vice-Chairman, on behalf of the Board wished Mr S. Longson every good wish for his proposed visit to the West Indies.

Editor's Comments

14th February: The home game against Stoke City saw a depleted Derby team take the field, with six first team regulars missing through injury. The Crystal Palace Manager, Bert Head, complained that Derby should have asked for the game to be postponed as there were several other games postponed throughout the season when other clubs had a similar injury list. His concern was that both Crystal Palace and Stoke City were fighting relegation and Stoke playing against a weakened team was unfair, backed up by 0–3 result. Head accused the Derby Manager of cheating and 'my team are bitterly angry'.

Thursday 22nd February 1973

Minute 6940 Manager's Report

The Manager, Mr B. H. Clough came into the Meeting and announced the proposed Team for the Cup tie with Queen's Park Rangers.

A request had been received from Mickleover Royal British Legion FC for a donation in respect of their Player Andrew Rowland who had recently been signed full-time professional by the Club. After discussion it was agreed that a cheque for £75 be forwarded to this Junior Club.

Minute 6941 Bass Charrington Advert

The Secretary confirmed recent discussions with Bass Charrington in respect of Ground Advertising Boards and after discussion it was agreed that the sum of £1,000 per board per annum be accepted and that a Contract for a two-year period be prepared.

Minute 6942 Football League Liner

The Secretary confirmed that after discussion with the Football League, the Club had managed to book the Football League's Official Train for our League match with Arsenal on March 31st 1973. The Train would be run through Derby County Promotions as usual and it was hoped that the Directors and possibly the Team would return on the Train.

Minute 6943 BBC Television

It was confirmed that the BBC Television would cover the home game v. Leeds United on 3rd March 1973.

Minute 6944 Sinfin Sports Ground

Mr F. W. Innes outlined further discussions he had had with the Corporation in respect of the recent approval of planning permission for industrial use and after discussion, it was agreed to the possible advertising of this property nationally and also the possibility of asking for Tenders. It was agreed, however, that the matter be further discussed at length at the next Meeting.

Minute 6945 Mr J. Kirkland

Mr S. C. Bradley read out a letter he had received from Mr J. Kirkland in respect of his application to join the Board of Directors. After discussion it was agreed that the letter be acknowledged and that the matter be discussed at the first Meeting following the Chairman's return from Holiday.

Minute 6946 European Cup Quarter-Final v. Spartak Trnava

The Secretary outlined travelling details for both the Official Party and supporters who will be travelling to Czechoslovakia via Vienna for the forthcoming quarter-final of the European Cup.

Minute 6947 Balance at Bank

The overdrawn balance at the Bank to date stood at £42,000 and the credit balance on the Promotions stood at £3,500.

Editor's Comments

24th February: The ticket prices for the European Cup quarter-final tie were announced and showed an increase on previous rounds. Seat ticket prices had risen by 25p and terrace tickets by 10p, raising them to £1.75 and 70p respectively. Sam Longson explained that the Board had deliberated for a long time on the right level of pricing and a detailed review of all English teams' prices in European competition was undertaken, and the new prices were still less than Leeds United charged for their semi-final three years earlier and still less than any other club left in the competition. The additional revenue would allow Derby to compete with their European counterparts, as well as the big city clubs in England who had bigger stadiums and could attract larger crowds.

4th March: The party of players and Directors left for the European Cup game against Spartak Trnava with an overnight stay at a hotel near Heathrow airport prior to a morning flight to Vienna, from where they would face a three-hour-long coach journey to Trnava. They would return to Vienna immediately after the match and fly back to the UK on the Thursday morning, 8th March.

Thursday 15th March 1973

A letter was read from the Chairman extending good wishes to the Board and wishing the Club every success for the coming FA Cup tie with Leeds and the European Cup tie v. Spartak Trnava.

Minute 6949 Bass Worthington

The Secretary confirmed that the Contract for a two-year period commencing 1st August 1973 would be drawn up with the Brewery at £1,000 per Board per annum. It was also confirmed that Bass Worthington would pay the Club £1,000 in respect of the two boards from 1st January 1973 to 31st July 1973.

Minute 6951 Balance at Bank

The Club's overdrawn balance at the Bank stood at £20,500 with £2,500 credit on the Promotions Account.

Minute 6952 European Cup, Quarter-Final v. Spartak Trnava

The Chairman, on behalf of the Board, congratulated the Manager on the Team's fine efforts in Trnava in the away leg of the European Cup quarter-final and it was also requested that it be recorded that congratulations be offered to the Secretary for arranging the trip to Czechoslovakia.

Discussion took place regarding the possible increase of European Bonuses for the Playing Staff over and above their Contractual agreement of £200 per game. It was agreed that the matter be discussed in conjunction with the Manager at a later date and that subject to Football League and Treasury Sanction, these increases would be included in new Contracts for the players for Season 1973–74.

Minute 6953 Sinfin Lane Sports Ground

It was proposed by Mr F. W. Innes that the sale of Sinfin Lane would be put up for sale by Tender. This proposition was seconded by Sir Robertson King, KBE and the following details agreed.

Closing date for accepting Tenders – 23rd June 1973

Special Board Meeting to discuss Tenders – 28th June 1973

Completion date for financial arrangements – 5th August 1973

Minute 6954 Raynesway Sports Ground

The Secretary confirmed that a verbal tender from Messrs Perks & Co. in respect of new training facilities at Raynesway of £21,000 had been received. It was agreed that although this was an estimated figure, it was acceptable and that the Club would await a written tender before officially confirming their acceptance.

Minute 6955 FA Cup – Trainer/Coach Staff Bonuses

It was agreed that the following Bonuses be paid to the following in respect of the FA Cup ties to date.

J. Gordon £150 (four games x £37.50 per game)

G. Guthrie £100 (four games x £25 per game)

J. Sheridan £100 (four games x £25 per game)

Minute 6956 Crush Barriers

The Secretary confirmed that the Football Association's Structural Architects would be visiting the Ground on Tuesday, 27th March at 10.00 a.m. to test the crush barriers within the Ground. The Secretary confirmed that the Borough Architect and Local Police would be in attendance.

Minute 6957 Manager's Report

The Manager, Mr B. H. Clough came into the Meeting and reported on relevant team matters and the Club's injury position at the present moment.

It was confirmed that Stephen Powell had been fined £20 for a breach of Club Disciplinary Rules.

Minute 6958 FA Cup Pool

It was reported that the Club had received £3,400 being the distribution of the FA Cup Pool up to and including the Third, Fourth and Fifth Rounds of the FA Cup.

Minute 6959 Television – FA Cup Sixth Round v. Leeds United

It was confirmed that ITV would be televising the Cup tie on Saturday v. Leeds United and a fixed sum of £250 would be received by Derby County Football Club.

Minute 6960 Midland Intermediate League Challenge Cup Final

It was confirmed that the away Leg of this Cup Final at Stoke would now be played on Wednesday 18th April 1973 and not as previously arranged on 25th April.

Editor's Comments

EUROPEAN CUP Quarter-Final FINANCIAL BREAKDOWN

GROSS RECEIPTS		EXPENSES	
Gate	34,000	Referee & Linesmen	300
TV Fees	7,500	Checkers	350
		Advertising	450
		Police	500
		Floodlights	25
		Presents	250
		UEFA 3%	1,000
		UEFA TV 10%	750
		Away Game	
		Hotel Sarajevo	700
		Aircraft	3,000
		Profit (approx.)	33,175
	41,500		41,500

Profit approx.	£33,175
Deduct Bonuses for entry into Europe	
Manager	£3,000
Assistant Manager	£3,000
Players 18 x £200 = £3,600	
Approximate Net Profit	£23,575

Monday 26ᵗʰ March 1973

Minute 6962 Sinfin Lane Sports Ground

Mr F. W. Innes gave a progress report on the development of Sinfin Lane and will be preparing the necessary form of Tender in conjunction with Mr Rudd for submission to the Board at a future meeting.

Minute 6963 Balance at Bank

The Club's overdrawn balance at the Bank was £4,000 overdrawn with the Promotions Account being in credit at present at £1,500.

Minute 6964 European Cup Semi-Final v. Juventus

General discussion took place regarding the travel details of our proposed trip to Italy for the semi-final of the European Cup and after discussion the following prices were confirmed.

"B" Stand & Ley Stand Centre	£3
All other seating	£2.50
Osmaston, Normanton & Paddock	£1.25
Popular Side	£1

The Secretary confirmed to the Meeting that tickets would go on sale before the first leg tie in Juventus.

Minute 6965 Peter Taylor Bonuses

A request from the Assistant Manager, Peter Taylor in respect of his outstanding bonuses to be paid in respect of the quarter-final of the European Cup v. Spartak Trnava (£3,000) and the Sixth Round of the FA Cup v. Q.P.R. (£1,500).

It was agreed that this Bonus totalling £4,500 be paid.

Minute 6966 J. Kirkland, ESQ.

It was agreed that a letter be forwarded to Mr Kirkland explaining that the proposed meeting re. his Directorship of the Company would now have to be postponed due to the regrettable illness of the Chairman. It was also agreed two Box Tickets be forwarded to Mr Kirkland for each Game to the end of the Season.

Minute 6967 Manager's Report

The Manager, Mr B. H. Clough came into the Meeting and reported on relevant Team matters and that the injuries sustained by Hinton and Hennessey could rule them out for the rest of the season. It was hoped, however, that Hinton's would perhaps be fit for the 2nd Leg of the European Cup semi-final.

Discussion took place regarding European Cup Bonuses and it was agreed that the following additional payments would be made to the playing staff in respect of the European Cup quarter-final, semi-final and Final ties. These figures to be included in the Contracts for Season 1973–74 and to be paid after 1st July 1973.

£175 each for playing in Quarter-final

£550 each for playing in Semi-final

£800 each for playing in Final

£500 each for winning Final

These aforementioned bonuses only apply to the 12 Players taking part in the match but the original £200 already in existing Contracts, will be paid to the 16 nominated for the game.

Editor's Comments

Sunday 8th April saw the official Derby party leave East Midlands Airport for a direct flight to Turin to face the Italian footballing giants of Juventus for the first leg of the European Cup semi-final. The return flight was booked for Wednesday evening straight after the game and scheduled to arrive back in Derby around 11 p.m.

A 1–3 defeat was not the result Derby would have wanted, but it could have been much worse and they were grateful for the Kevin Hector goal and the knowledge that Alan Hinton could be fit enough to play an important part in the return leg. They would have to play the home game without Gemmill and McFarland, because of controversial bookings in the first game. Gemmill had his name taken for a trip on Furino, retaliation after Furino's elbow had made deliberate contact with his face. McFarland's booking was very strange. He jumped with Cuccureddu for a high ball and the two heads clashed and he was booked. As both players had already been booked in the competition (in the matches against Spartak in the previous round), this meant an automatic one-match ban, which meant they would have to sit out the return leg at the Baseball Ground. Furino would also miss the return, but his prolonged kicking and fouling of Gemmill all over the field should have ended in more punishment than a booking.

As the Derby *Evening Telegraph* described it, 'It looked like a put-up job.'

It was only after the game that the full drama of the goings-on behind the scenes became public knowledge. Peter Taylor originally raised alarm bells even before the kick-off when he came into the dressing room saying, 'Haller's in with the ref again. That's twice I've seen him.'

At half-time Haller, only named as a substitute, walked off with referee Gerhard Schulenburg instead of his teammates. Peter Taylor followed them and got an elbow in the ribs from Haller, and a large group of stewards and police stopped Taylor and tried to arrest him before he managed to get to the safety of the Derby dressing room. John Charles, still highly respected by the Juventus supporters, calmed the incident down but by then Taylor had missed the half-time interval.

This, together with the strange bookings for McFarland and Gemmill, caused Brian Clough to explode with rage after the game. Clough wrote in his autobiography, 'I couldn't believe my eyes at some of the things that happened in Turin. We had two key players booked well before half-time … As far as I can remember their only crime was to stand somewhere adjacent to an opponent who flung himself on the floor. Now wasn't that a coincidence? McFarland and Gemmill – two players who just happened to have been booked in previous games – would now, automatically, be ruled out of the second leg. It stank to high heaven. I'd heard lurid tales of bribery, corruption, the bending of match officials in Italy, call it what you will, but I'd never before seen what struck me as clear evidence. I went barmy.'

Brian Glanville from the *Sunday Times* spoke fluent Italian, and was ordered by Clough to translate for the Italian press the following: 'No cheating bastards will I talk to, I will not talk to any cheating bastards!' This met with a predictably hostile response. An official complaint was made to UEFA about the referee's handling of the game, but after an inquiry, no apparent action was taken.

Tuesday 17ᵗʰ April 1973

Minute 6968 Manager's Report

The Manager, Mr B. H. Clough came into the Meeting and reported on the Club's present injury position and the possible team for Saturday.

It was confirmed that Boulton had been suspended for two matches following incidents after the Leeds United League game at the Baseball Ground on Saturday

3rd March. Mr M. Keeling represented the Club at the Commission together with Ron Webster who attended as a witness. Boulton had also been fined £100 by the Club for this action.

Minute 6969 Raynesway Sports Ground

It was agreed that confirmation of the written estimate of £21,000 be accepted and it was agreed that work commence at the earliest convenience. It was also confirmed that a small medical room would be incorporated in the existing framework of the building.

Minute 6970 Sinfin Lane Sports Ground

Mr F. W. Innes confirmed that the Club had received a written offer from Evans of Leeds of £87,500 for the site. After discussion, it was agreed that at the moment, this offer be refused and that the Club pursue the course of appealing on behalf of the Council's refusal for residential development and that the matter be discussed again at a later date when the appeal has been considered by the Corporation.

Minute 6971 Balance at Bank

The Club's account to date stood at £20,000 credit with a further donation of £5,000 having been received from Derby County Promotions. To date, Derby County Promotions had donated £55,000, to the Football Club's General Account. It was agreed that in view of the Club's present financial position, Season ticket money would be placed on deposit.

Minute 6972 The Football League Limited – Pools Agreement

Discussion took place in respect of the Football League's recent announcement of the Agreement signed for the next thirteen years with the Pools Promoters Association for a figure of £2,000,000 per year.

After discussion, it was agreed that the Secretary write and express the Club's views to the League in respect of the Club's disappointment at the outcome of the negotiations and in particular, in the way negotiations had been handled by the League.

Minute 6973 Season tickets 1973–74

After general discussion, it was agreed that the basic price of Season tickets for the coming season would remain the same as last year, 1972–73, but Value Added Tax would be added in all cases.

Value Added Tax would also be added to single match admissions and these would be as follows for the coming Season.

'B' Stand & Ley Stand Centre	£1.25	10%	£1.40
Ley Wings 'A' & 'C' Stand	£1	10%	£1.10
Osmaston & Normanton Stands 80p	10%	90p	
Osmaston/Normanton			
& Paddock Terracing	50p	10%	55p
Popular Side Terracing	40p	10%	45p

It was agreed that once again, four Cup vouchers would be included in the majority of seat Season ticket books and that sales would commence during the early part of May. The usual letter to Season ticket holders would be distributed at the turnstiles prior to the game v. Ipswich Town on 30th April.

Minute 6974 Playing Area - The Baseball Ground

It was agreed that again Cambridge Soil Services Limited would treat the pitch during the Close Season with soil injection. It was confirmed that the total cost of this would be £1,386 and that work would commence during the early part of May.

Minute 6975 The Ram

Following discussion, it was confirmed that the Club would again produce a Club Newspaper for season 1973–74. The price would be 8p.

Minute 6976 Ground Advertising

The Secretary outlined details of an Agreement with the Bank of Italy for Ground Advertising for the return leg at the Baseball Ground of the European Cup semi-final. It was agreed that $10,000 would be paid to the Club for perimeter advertising.

Editor's Comments

The two-match ban on Colin Boulton imposed by the FA Disciplinary Committee prompted Clough to comment, 'I am absolutely staggered that Boulton, who has never been in trouble before, should get the same treatment as players with records as long as your arm.' Boulton was found guilty of bringing the game into disrepute for allegedly rubbing a dirty glove into the face of the referee as they left the field after the Leeds United Cup tie.

On 29th March a letter was received from UEFA regarding the limited press facilities at the Baseball Ground. The usual facilities catered for 30 journalists and this had been extended to over 60 by utilising additional space behind the dugouts. The letter suggested that even this number would be inadequate for the arrival of Juventus. The example quoted on the letter was the recent Ajax v. Bayern semi-final game where over 200 press places were required.

The overall winners of the tie would go through to the Final that was to be played in Belgrade on 30th May, with a 8.30 p.m. kick-off at the Crvana Zvezda stadium. A possible replay date was also fixed for two days later at the same venue.

Ticket prices were increased again for this game – £3 for seats in the B Stand and Ley Stand Centre and £1 for a terrace ticket on the Popside.

ITV had exclusive broadcast rights on the game, being allowed to show 45 minutes after 10.30 p.m. The fee was £7,000, plus any revenue from sales throughout Europe (Italian TV would be charged £3,000 and any others £1,000).

Player bonuses for reaching the Final and winning had been agreed – £800 playing, and additional £500 for winning the competition.

Francisco Marques Lobo, the Portuguese referee for the second leg, reported to his FA that an Italian agent (former referee Deso Solti and 'fixer') had offered him a bribe to favour Juventus – a UEFA sub-committee inquiry in Zurich didn't even bother to interview the main parties involved and took no action and Juventus proceeded to the Final. UEFA did, however, suspend Solti indefinitely. Over a year after the semi-final matches, the *Sunday Times* (Brian Glanville and Keith Botsford) interviewed Lobo and printed the bribery story (known as the Lobo-Solti case), which did not go down well in Italy. It was not until 2006 that the Italian FA stepped in and finally punished Juventus and several other top-flight clubs with serial match fixing going back years. Juventus were to suffer the harshest punishment, being relegated to Serie B, a 30-point deduction and being stripped of two League titles.

Thursday 3rd May 1973

Minute 6978 Manager's Report

The Manager, Mr B. H. Clough came into the Meeting and confirmed that there would be no change in the First Team to play Wolverhampton Wanderers in the final game of the Season at the Baseball Ground on Friday evening.

The Manager announced to the Board that no Players would in fact be released from Contracts this year and that all Players would be retained.

Details of proposed tours were confirmed and it was agreed that the Team would fly out for a 10-day tour of Majorca commencing Saturday 5th May with one game v. Son Servera on Saturday 12th May 1973. The Party will return to England on Tuesday 14th May.

It was confirmed that a pre-season tour of Germany and Spain would take place during the month of August 1973.

It was hoped the Team would leave England on Sunday 12th August and play FC Osnabruck on the 14th. The Party would then fly to Spain on the 15th and stay in Spain for five days playing two matches on the 18th and 19th returning to England on the morning of the 20th.

At the present time, it was hoped to play the Alan Durban Testimonial Fund game at the Baseball Ground on Monday evening, 20th August.

The Manager confirmed that Roger Davies had been fined £100 for a breach of Club Disciplinary Rules in respect of being sent off in the European Cup semi-final v. Juventus.

Minute 6979 Training Staff Bonuses

The following bonuses were confirmed in respect of the European Cup quarter-final and semi-final ties for the Training Staff.

J. Gordon – £250

J. Sheridan – £125

G. Guthrie – £125

Minute 6980 Balance at Bank

The Club's credit balance on the current account stood at £25,000 to date with a cheque due to Leicester City in respect of the transfer of David Nish.

Minute 6981 Promotions Organiser

It was agreed by the Board of Directors that the recommendation from the Promotions Committee be accepted that Stuart Robinson be appointed to the new position of Commercial Executive for Derby County Promotions. The vacancy being caused by the departure of Stuart Crooks to take up a similar position with Leicester City Football Club. It was agreed that salary and commission be left in the hands of the Promotions Committee to finalise.

It was agreed that a letter of appreciation be forwarded to Stuart Crooks for his efforts on behalf of the Club over the past 10 years.

Minute 6982 Football League Limited – Rule 40A

It was confirmed that the Club's Account had been credited with £11,490 in respect of the refund from the Football League Pool for signing on fees.

Minute 6983 Football League Limited – Regulation 31

It was confirmed that the Club would propose an alteration to Rule 31 in that we would put forward at the Annual General Meeting of the Football League in June 1973, the proposition for four up and four down.

Minute 6984 Staff Wages

It was agreed that as from the 1st May, the following Ground Staff would receive a £1 plus 4% rounding up to the nearest 50p.

A. Cleaver

Barry Clough

B. Hill

R. Martin

C. Notley

It was agreed that recommendations from the Secretary in respect of the Administration would be discussed at the next Board Meeting.

Editor's Comments

4th May: A 3–0 win on the last match of the season against Wolverhampton Wanderers saw them finish in 7th place and needed a favour from Leeds United for them to qualify for the following season's UEFA Cup. For that to happen, Leeds had to win the FA Cup Final (v. Sunderland) or European Cup Winners Cup Final (v. AC Milan).

David Nish was away on holiday in Majorca when he got a late call from Sir Alf Ramsey for his availability to play in the British Home Internationals against Northern Ireland on 12th May at Goodison Park, Everton. He was soon replaced for the remaining matches in the tournament and the other internationals during the summer by Emlyn Hughes, who missed the Northern Ireland game as Liverpool were in UEFA Cup Final action.

Tuesday 22ⁿᵈ May 1973

On behalf of the Board of Directors, Mr T. W. Rudd expressed delight to see the Chairman, Mr S. Longson, back in the Chair following his recent illness and wished him all the best wishes for the future.

Minute 6986 Manager's Report

The Assistant Manager, Mr Peter Taylor came into the Meeting and reported on relevant Team matters during the past weeks.

It was reported that the end of the season Tour had gone quite successfully and that the Team beat Son Severa by six goals to nil.

Anthony Parry had been sent home from the Tour for Disciplinary matters and necessary action will be taken during the Close Season.

Details of the Official Party representing the Club in the Four Day International Youth Tournament in Dusseldorf were confirmed and it was confirmed that no Director would be travelling with the Party.

It was agreed that additional payment be made in respect of the Training and Coaching Staff for the European Cup successes last Season.

J. Gordon be paid an additional £400

J. Sheridan be paid an additional £200

G. Guthrie be paid an additional £200

Minute 6987 Balance at Bank

The Club's overdrawn balance at the Bank to date stood at £3,000 with £50,000 at present being on Deposit in respect of Season tickets.

Minute 6988 Sinfin Lane Sports Ground

Mr F. W. Innes reported that discussion had been held with prepared purchasers for Sinfin and that offers in excess of £100,000 were being discussed.

He hoped that for the next Meeting he would have a concrete written offer in respect of this Site to place before the Board.

Minute 6989 Raynesway Sports Ground

The Secretary confirmed that Perks were now in a position to commence work on the new Dressing Rooms and a further progress report would be available for the next Meeting.

It was also confirmed that the Steward had terminated his employment with the Company.

Minute 6990 Football League Annual General Meeting

Discussion took place in respect of various proposed alterations to Rules for the forthcoming Football League Annual General Meeting.

It was confirmed that the Chairman would address the Meeting at length on the Club's proposal for four up and four down.

Minute 6991 Club Minibus

An application from A. Cleaver for the loan of the Club Minibus for a two-week period for personal use was refused.

Minute 6992 Crush Barriers

The Secretary outlined that the final phase of barrier construction was now underway and that new barriers would be installed on parts of the Normanton Terracing and Popular Side.

Minute 6993 A. S. Webb – Secretary

It was agreed that the Secretary's Salary be increased to £5,000 per annum with effect from 1st May 1973.

Minute 6994 J. Kirkland, ESQ.

It was proposed by the Chairman, MrS. Longson and seconded by the President, Sir Robertson King, KBE, and unanimously agreed that Mr J. Kirkland be appointed to the Board of Directors of the Company as from this date and be invited to attend the next Meeting of the Directors.

Friday 22nd June 1973

On behalf of the Board, the Chairman, Mr S. Longson, welcomed Mr J. Kirkland to the Directorate and wished him a long and successful association with the Club. Mr Kirkland suitably responded.

Minute 6996 Manager's Report

The Manager, Mr B. H. Clough came into the Meeting and reported on relevant Team matters over the past weeks.

The Manager reported that offers had been made for the following three Players – Peter Daniel, Alan Durban and Alan Lewis and that in all cases, the offers had been rejected.

It was confirmed that Roger Davies would be suspended from the next three games with the Club for any UEFA Tournament in respect of him being sent off in the European Cup semi-final v. Juventus.

It was also reported that Terry Hennessey had undergone an operation on his Achilles Tendon and that at the moment he was in heavy plaster. It was understood that it would be well into the month of September next before he would be in a position to resume playing. The Secretary outlined that an Insurance Claim was in hand with the Football League and the Club were receiving a percentage of his weekly salary during the weeks of incapacity.

The Secretary outlined details of the proposed Pre-Season Tour of Germany and Spain and confirmed that the Party would be departing Derby on Saturday 11th August 1973 and returning to Derby on Monday 20th August 1973. Two games would be involved, v. Osnabruck on 14th August 1973 and two games in an International Tournament in Huelva, Spain on 18th and 19th August.

Terms for these games as follows:

£3,000 v. Osnabruck

£10,000 Spanish Tournament

£13,000

These fees subject to Agent's Commission 10% (Gunter Bachmann). For the Spanish Tournament, all travelling expenses and hotel would be paid for, for a Party of 22 persons.

It was confirmed that the Club would not accept the invitation from the Football League to enter the Texaco Cup next Season 1973–74.

Minute 6997 Sinfin Lane

Mr F. W. Innes reported that on behalf of the Board he had negotiated the sale of Sinfin Lane to Evans of Leeds for a sum of £135,000. Completion date being 31st December 1973 or before that date subject to four weeks' notice being given by Derby County. It was estimated that an approximate Capital Gains figure of £30,000 could be paid leaving £100,000 clear profit to the Football Club.

On behalf of the Board, the Chairman, Mr Longson congratulated Mr Innes and Mr Rudd on their efforts in negotiating both the purchasing of Raynesway Sports Ground and the sale of Sinfin Lane.

Minute 6998 Balance at Bank

The Secretary reported that the Club's current account to date stood at £6,272 in credit, the Ordinary Deposit Account at 6.5% interest stood at £13,500 and the special monthly Deposit Account at 8.5% interest at £200,000.

Minute 6999 Season ticket Sales 1973–74

Season ticket sales to date had reached a gross figure of £270,000.

Minute 7000 'B' Stand Re-Sheeting

It was confirmed that F. Dysons & Sons of Huddersfield would be commencing work during the early part of July on the re-sheeting of 'B' Stand. The price being £4,297 for 'B' Stand and £864 for the Osmaston Stand Gable End.

Minute 7001 Invitations

Invitations had been received in respect of the Scottish FA and Liverpool Football Club to attend Celebration Dinners.

It was agreed that the Chairman and Mrs Longson attend the Liverpool Banquet and it was left to the Secretary to organise a suitable representative to attend the function in Scotland.

Editor's Comments

The appointment of Jack Kirkland to the Board of Directors was a politically motivated move by the Board, as they had suffered criticism from Kirkland in the past and, as the largest shareholder (approximately 21%), he could make life difficult for them. By allowing him to join the Board, he could no longer make any public comments criticising the Directors.

On 26th June 1973 the Management team met England World Cup winning captain Bobby Moore at the Churchill Hotel, London without knowledge of the Chairmen of either club and the Manager of West Ham United, Ron Greenwood, with a view to signing for Derby. This would be classed as strictly against Football League rules (17 and 61) and would have put the Club in a great deal of trouble had the football authorities found out. Discussions went to such a degree that all personal terms and arrangements for training, et cetera, had been agreed.

Clough, however, claimed that the expenses incurred for the trip were to entertain the parents of a boy whom the club might be interested in signing.

Having survived the gross negligence/administrative issues of 1970, and the Ian Moore transfer debacle of 1972, the Chairman was so worried about the consequences of breaking the rules once again that Longson dictated a letter (he was ill in Anglesey) to all Directors informing them of the situation, and that he did not agree with the Manager's conduct and forbade him to continue with any further discussions with Moore.

The prospect of having a defensive line of Todd, McFarland, Moore and Nish and potentially Shilton in goal was an intriguing one. When a formal approach was denied by West Ham United, Clough ensured that the national newspapers were aware of Derby's interest in an attempt to unsettle the player or put pressure on the West Ham Manager to sell him.

	HOME			AWAY	

League Diision 1

19/08/1972	Chelsea	1–2	12/08/1972	Southampton	1–1
23/08/1972	Manchester City	1–0	15/08/1972	Crystal Palace	0–0
02/09/1972	Liverpool	2–1	26/08/1972	Norwich City	0–1
16/09/1972	Birmingham City	1–0	29/08/1972	Everton	0–1
30/09/1972	Tottenham Hotspur	2–1	09/09/1972	West Bromwich Albion	1–2
14/10/1972	Leicester City	2–1	23/09/1972	Manchester United	0–3
28/10/1972	Sheffield United	2–1	07/10/1972	Leeds United	0–5
11/11/1972	Crystal Palace	2–2	21/10/1972	Ipswich Town	1–3
25/11/1972	Arsenal	5–0	04/11/1972	Manchester City	0–4
09/12/1972	Coventry City	2–0	18/11/1972	West Ham United	2–1
16/12/1972	Newcastle United	1–1	02/12/1972	Wolverhampton Wanderers	2–1
26/12/1972	Manchester United	3–1	23/12/1972	Stoke City	0–4
06/01/1973	Norwich City	1–0	30/12/1972	Chelsea	1–1
27/01/1973	West Bromwich Albion	2–0	20/01/1973	Liverpool	1–1
14/02/1973	Stoke City	0–3	10/02/1973	Birmingham City	0–2
17/02/1973	Southampton	4–0	28/02/1973	Newcastle United	0–2
03/03/1973	Leeds United	2–3	10/03/1973	Leicester City	0–0
21/04/1973	West Ham United	1–1	24/03/1973	Sheffield United	1–3
28/04/1973	Everton	3–1	31/03/1973	Arsenal	1–0
30/04/1973	Ipswich Town	3–0	14/04/1973	Coventry City	2–0
04/05/1973	Wolverhampton Wanderers	3–0	18/04/1973	Tottenham Hotspur	0–1

League Cup

| 06/10/1972 | Chelsea | 0–0 | 05/09/1972 | Swindon Town | 1–0 |
| | | | 09/10/1972 | Chelsea | 2–3 |

FA Cup

03/02/1973	Tottenham Hotspur	1–1	13/01/1973	Peterborough United	1–0
24/02/1973	QPR	4–2	07/02/1973	Tottenham Hotspur	5–3 aet
17/03/1973	Leeds United	0–1			

European Cup

13/09/1972	FK Želzeni ar	2–0	29/09/1971	FK Želzeni ar	2–1
23/10/1972	Benfica	3–0	03/11/1971	Benfica	0–0
21/03/1973	Spartak Trnava	2–0	08/12/1971	Spartak Trnava	0–1
25/04/1973	Juventus	0–0	11/04/1973	Juventus	1–3

Friendlies

05/08/1972	FC Den Haag	1–2	26/07/1972	FC Den Haag	1–1
			29/07/1972	FC Tilburg	2–1
			01/08/1972	Schalke 04	2–0
			08/08/1972	Scarborough	1–3

Testimonial

| | | | 27/11/1972 | Luton Town (Buxton) | 1–0 |

SEASON SUMMARY

Football League Division One:	7th
FA Cup:	Sixth Round
Football League Cup:	Third Round
European Cup:	Semi-final
Average League Attendance:	29,765
Highest Attendance:	38,462 v. Leeds United, Division One
Top League Scorers:	Hector (14)
	Hinton (13)

SEASON 1973-74

Tuesday 17th July 1973

Minute 7004 Manager's Report

Both the Manager and Assistant Manager came into the Meeting and reported on relevant team matters.

It was reported that the Football League Cover for Players Insurance had been increased to £256,000 for season 1973–74 and that the Club would take additional Insurance cover of £2,110,000 on our players at an approximate cost of £21,000.

It was confirmed that Colin Boulton had now re-signed and that the two outstanding contracts for Kevin Hector and Alan Hinton would be completed within the next few days.

It was reported that excellent progress was being made by both the injured players, Hennessey and Davies.

Minute 7005 Sinfin Lane Sports Ground

It was reported that Derby Corporation still held a Debenture on Sinfin through the loan in respect of Ley Stand.

After discussion it was agreed that should the Corporation refuse to release the land then the outstanding amount of £22,500 be repaid to the Corporation forthwith.

Minute 7006 Balance at Bank

The Club's credit balance at the Bank to date stood at:

Current Account	£5,300
Promotions Account	£4,000
Deposit Account	£23,000
Special Deposit Account	£200,000

Minute 7007 Season tickets – Season 1973–74

Season ticket sales to date in respect of Season 1973–74 stood at £306,000.

Minute 7008 Raynesway – Tractor

It was confirmed that the Club would purchase a second-hand tractor for use at Raynesway Sports ground. Mr J. Kirkland and the Secretary would finalise details.

Minute 7009 Burnley Football Club – Dinner

It was agreed that the Club be represented at Burnley FC 2nd Division Championship Dinner to be held at Blackpool on Tuesday 24th July 1973.

Minute 7010 Football League – National Spot the Ball Competition

The Secretary outlined the Football League proposals for organising jointly with Ladbrokes Limited a National Competition for all Clubs. Promotions Agents would be involved and an estimated 45% of Gross Takings would be refunded to Clubs, i.e.

Agents 15% Commission

Clubs   30%

     45%

Editor's Comments

An Emergency Committee meeting of the Football Association preferred a charge of misconduct against Manager Brian Clough for breach of rule 40a, in respect of remarks which had appeared in the *Sunday Express* on 5th August 1973. His latest outburst came about when Leeds United were given a suspended fine of just £3,000 for consistently bringing the game into disrepute by the FA Disciplinary Commission, with Clough suggesting that they should be demoted to the Second Division, as the FA had called them one of the dirtiest clubs in Britain and Revie must take responsibility for that. 'The befuddled minds of the men who run the game have missed the most marvellous chance of cleaning up soccer in one swoop,' Clough added. 'The trouble with football's disciplinary system is that those who sat in judgment being officials of other clubs might well have a vested interest.'

Clough was in contract discussions with London Weekend Television (LWT) worth £15,000 per year to appear on their *On the Ball* programme, replacing Jimmy Hill who had switched to the BBC to host their flagship football programme, *Match of the Day* on Saturday evenings. This was to be filmed in London, typically on a Wednesday or Thursday, sometimes on Friday, and back again on Sunday for a highlights show. This inevitably would mean that he would not be present for some of the team's preparation for the weekend fixture at the most important time of the week. The Directors were not at all happy with this arrangement, as he also had agreements to write a weekly newspaper article, other public appearances, TV shows (e.g. Parkinson) and he was also a Labour Party member and would readily lend his support to them as well.

Sam Longson was increasingly frustrated with the situation: 'It has come to the stage when the constant threats of Brian leaving Derby have to be settled once and for all. It is time Brian made up his mind what he wants to do and to get on and do it. If he decides that he wants to get out of soccer to give himself a free platform to speak his mind about the FA, Leeds United and just about everybody else, then I for one won't stand in his way.'

Derby were still looking out for some big money transfers (one of which was targeted as Bobby Moore), which, if they were to happen, would, according to the Manager, make Derby 'certs to win the League for the second time in three years'. They were handed a boost ahead of pre-season when Roger Davies (cartilage operation) and Terry Hennessey (Achilles tendon) were both expected to be fully fit for the start of the season.

Tuesday 31st July 1973

The club's Annual Report and Accounts showed the following shareholding amongst the Directors when the financial year end closed on 31st July 1973.

	31st July 1973	1st August 1972
Sir Robertson King, KBE	50	50
S. Longson	1,325	1,325
S. C. Bradley	1,371	1,371
T. W. Rudd	1,210	1,210
F. W. Innes	1,260	1,260
F. B. Walters (died 30/11/72)	-	1,235
M. Keeling	91	91
J. Kirkland (appointed 22/5/73)	4,247	-

The Revenue Account shows that the gate receipts generated from the European Cup matches amounted to £135,211 (significantly more than receipts from all other matches put together) and TV and broadcasting fees had more than trebled from £15,654 during the Championship season to £50,506. Season ticket receipts had increased by nearly 32% to £320,632 but that obviously meant that normal gate receipts would fall, totalling £108,726.

Other revenue streams had also risen sharply as a result of the success. Advertising revenue had doubled to £27,909 and sales of *The Ram* newspaper/programme had nearly trebled to £11,168.

The Expenditure was broadly the same between the two years with a couple of exceptions. Wages and salaries had decreased by £10,000, Travelling and Match Expenses had had risen by £35,000 and Legal and Professional Charges had gone from £405 in 1972 to £8,575 in 1973.

Transfers showed that the Club had spent more than they had received for players during the previous 12 months, which amounted to £105,721.

This balanced out to show a surplus of £98,139 for the year, and with the donation from Derby County Promotions gave them a very healthy-looking balance to carry forward of £166,487, compared to the previous year's balance of £5,348.

Summarised Revenue Account

	1973 (£)	1972 (£)
Match Receipts	564,569	427,426
Advertising	27,909	13,608
Ram Newspaper	11,168	4,920
TV, Broadcasting	50,506	15,654
Interest	**3,539**	**898**
Total Income	657,691	462,506
Expenditure		
Wages and Salaries	223,921	233,190
Travelling and match expenses	88,610	53,025
Rent, Rates, Insurance	25,042	15,648
Other Expenditure	116,258	109,615
Total Expenditure	453,831	411,478
Transfer fees paid less received	**105,721**	**23,995**
Total Expenditure	559,552	435,473
Surplus for Year	98,139	27,033
Add Derby County Promotions	63,000	60,000
Surplus Brought Forward	**5,348**	**(81,685)**
Balance Carried Forward	166,487	5,348

Monday 6ᵗʰ August 1973

Minute 7012 Manager's Report

The Manager, Mr B. H. Clough came into the Meeting and reported to the Board on relevant team matters. He reported that Hector and Hinton had signed new contracts and these had been posted on to the Football League.

It was agreed that a donation of £25 be forwarded to Jeff Farmer of the *Daily Mail* in respect of the Peter Ingall Fund.

Discussions took place regarding the availability of Raynesway and Dressing Room Accommodation and in was confirmed that the Builder had promised completion by the end of September at the latest.

Minute 7013 Season tickets 1973–74

Season ticket sales to date in respect of Season 1973–74 stood at £328,000.

Minute 7014 National Westminster Bank Limited

Mr S. Bradley outlined details of a Meeting he had with the Secretary and Mr Lowry, Manager, National Westminster Bank Limited in respect of the Club's future borrowing powers for the coming year. It was confirmed that an overdraft limit of £80,000 would be available under the present Directors' Guarantees. A further additional £20,000 would be available provided additional Guarantees were secured from the Directors.

After discussion, it was agreed than in view of the Club's present securities, a further meeting be arranged with Mr Lowry to seek a higher overdraft limit.

Minute 7015 BBC Television

It was confirmed that our first home match of the season, on Saturday 25th August would be included in BBC's *Match of The Day* programme.

Minute 7016 Pre-Season Tour of Germany & Spain

The Secretary confirmed financial details in respect of the proposed Pre-Season Tour of Germany and Spain and it was agreed that the Party would now travel on the Friday and stay overnight at the Grand Hotel, Manchester.

Editor's Comments

Tuesday 7th August 1973

A meeting in London between Clough and London Weekend Television's Head of Sport (John Bromley) and their leading football commentator Brian Moore took place in which they offered Clough the position as expert summariser and critic. Bromley said, 'it all depends on whether he wants to leave Derby and whether the Derby Board are prepared to let him go.'

Clough duly accepted a part-time position as a freelance member of the *On the Ball* and *The Big Match* programmes. The statement issued by LWT said, 'he is considering a full-time career in television subject to Derby County agreeing to release him. He has undertaken to inform LWT of his decision in two weeks.' Clough commented that, 'Whenever I make my decision about going full-time, the first person who will know will be Peter Taylor, then the players and finally the Board.'

Monday 20th August 1973

The possibility of the 32-year-old Bobby Moore leaving West Ham United was getting more newspaper coverage than ever before, with details suggesting that Derby had made an enquiry during the summer and were coming back with an offer in excess of £100,000 for him, and would also take Trevor Brooking as well as part of the deal. Moore himself showed a renewed interest in Derby's offer by talking directly to the press without consulting his own Manager, and was quoted as saying that he was no longer happy at the progress of the London club (they were second from bottom) and was coming under increasing pressure for his performances at club and international level.

Bobby Moore went to the press to share his feelings about the rejected Derby approach by West Ham United, saying, 'I was really surprised. It's a wonderful incentive for the new season to think a club as good as Derby should be keen to sign me. I look on it as the highest of compliments and, to tell the truth, I'm delighted.'

Thursday 23rd August 1973

Minute 7018 Manager's Report

The Chairman reported that, whilst at the Raynesway Ground at 8.30 p.m. on the previous evening, he received a request via Mr Rudd from the Manager, stating that the Manager required an immediate meeting that evening with his Assistant and the Board to discuss very important business, and should this meeting not be held, it could mean that the Manager and his Assistant would not be with the Club for the Chelsea match on Saturday.

The Chairman then discussed this matter with the rest of the Directors present, and decided that in view of the fact that a Board Meeting had been scheduled for 10 o'clock the following morning, irrespective of consequences, this matter could wait.

This was conveyed to the Manager and his Assistant, together with the fact that all the Directors had an appointment with the Promotions Executive and their Supporters at the Pennine Hotel.

The Chairman told the Manager that he and the Board would be pleased to discuss any matter with him the following morning.

The Chairman emphasised that he had no knowledge of whatever what was in the Manager's mind.

The Manager and his Assistant were then invited into the Board Room, and asked to state their important business.

The Manager stated that he and his Assistant had fully discussed the matter, and they considered that the Board had gone sour on them, and would it not be far better if they shook hands and left in a proper and friendly manner and what in fact, was the feeling of the Board regarding this statement?

The Chairman explained that the Board had no feeling about matters going sour, but the Chairman further explained to the Manager in the strongest, in fact very strong terms, that both he and his Assistant were abusing their positions. They were cheating, and they were doing many things contrary to what would be expected of a good Manager, and that if he and his Assistant wanted to clear out, neither the Board nor he would raise any objections whatever.

The Chairman warned them that any further breach of FA Regulations or other rules would probably mean instant dismissal. In fact, he would have dismissed both of them immediately, had the Board agreed.

The Chairman asked terms, and the Manager immediately stated that these would have to be discussed later.

The Chairman went on to say that under no circumstances would he at present, dismiss the Manager or his Assistant, although the Manager had asked him to dismiss his Assistant some three weeks ago.

The Chairman also mentioned other domestic matters, which are not relevant to the Board, but he left no doubt in the Manager's mind that the Board were solidly behind him and that he intended to rule through strength, work absolutely to all rules and regulations, and that if the Manager or his Assistant did not like it, they had one alternative – that was to go.

The Chairman was quite clear and very blunt in all his statements.

He finalised by stating that he would be very sorry to see this happen, since he had both love and affection for the Manager, but he and the Board were fed up to the back teeth with his actions and creation of crises, which they would tolerate no more.

In closing, the Chairman asked the Manager to inform the Board in due course, of the details of his Agreement with ATV.

The Manager reported that Hennessey had been sent home to rest for two weeks and that Bailey had a cracked spine and could be out of action for a possible three or four weeks.

The Manager reported on various enquiries the Club had received in respect of Players O'Hare and Gemmill, but he confirmed that these offers were not acceptable to the Club.

Everton had advised the Club that Henry Newton was available for transfer, but the Manager had expressed that there was nothing concrete to report at the moment in this direction.

Minute 7019 Raynesway Sports Ground

Mr F. W. Innes and Mr J. Kirkland reported on their dissatisfaction at the progress of Raynesway Sports Ground and it was agreed that the Secretary write to F. Perks & Sons for detailed specification of work and that every effort be made to speed up the completion date.

Minute 7020 Sinfin Lane Sports Ground

Mr W. Rudd confirmed that he had applied for one month's completion for the sale of Sinfin and that this matter should now be resolved by the end of September.

Minute 7021 Season tickets 1973–74

The Secretary confirmed that Season ticket sales to date had reached £344,000.

Minute 7022 Balance at Bank

The credit balance on the Club's current account to date stood at £13,000 and the credit balance on the Club's deposit account stood at £16,800. The Club still had £200,000 on special deposit at a present rate of 11.5% which would be increased on 4th September 1973 to 13.25%.

It was also confirmed that the Secretary would place a further £20,000 on special deposit as from today's date.

Minute 7023 FA Disciplinary Procedures

The Secretary outlined Disciplinary Procedures for season 1973–74 and the relevant changes in the various rules.

It was confirmed that all Directors, Management and Players would be informed by letter of these changes at the request of the Football Association.

Minute 7024 Pre-Season Tour – Germany and Spain

The Secretary confirmed that the Gross Profit on the pre-season tour came to a total of £5,006 and out of that amount a figure of £1,123.80 would go to the Derbyshire Football Association and £500.60 to the FA, making a net profit to Derby County FC of £3,381.60.

Editor's Comments

As well as looking out for one or two big name signings, they would also have been interested in any youngsters that may have been available, but having scoured the country in the previous 18 months, the management could not identify anyone with the same potential as McFarland, Gemmill, Davies, et cetera.

More money had been spent on the stadium during the close season with the outside of the 'B' Stand being re-sheeted, the replacement of all of the crush barriers continued and the police had a purpose-built office and detention area constructed under the Osmaston Stand that allowed contact with the officers throughout the stadium.

12th September 1973

Alan Durban, signed from Cardiff City by Tim Ward in July 1963 for a fee of around £10,000, had left the Club for Shrewsbury Town. He had studied a football management course during the summer with ambitions to progress into team management and the opportunity at Shrewsbury was as a player/ Assistant Manager. In all he made 388 first team appearances, 15 as substitute, and scored 113 goals and won 27 Wales international caps. In his first game for Shrewsbury he scored one of the goals in a 2–0 win against Rochdale, their first victory of the season. He had been granted a testimonial game against Nottingham Forest which was to take place on 26th September.

There were to be a couple of experiments for the travelling Derby supporters – firstly, due to popularity of the service, there were going to be two Ramaway trains for each Saturday away game, each carrying 400 fans.

One would start at Burton and then call at Derby as usual, the second one would start at Alfreton and call at Long Eaton and Derby, depending upon the away location. For home fixtures, there was also a special train running from Alfreton to Derby via Long Eaton to help ease traffic congestion around the stadium area.

14th September 1973

The *Daily Mirror* reported that Derby were about to make an offer for one of the big signings they had wanted to make ever since the summer, this time Charlie George from Arsenal for a British transfer record of £300,000. There were no follow-up quotes to this from anyone, but it was known that Tottenham Hotspur and Liverpool were also tracking him, although as he was now first choice at Arsenal they would be reluctant to let him leave cheaply and this story quickly disappeared.

15th September 1973

Bobby Moore found himself at a crossroads and was clearly unsettled by the transfer speculation, and he was left out of the West Ham United team to play at Manchester United. He was due to meet with Ron Greenwood, his Manager, on Monday to determine his immediate future. The one medal Moore did not have in his collection was a First Division championship one – 'that would mean more to me than anything, even winning the World Cup again' – and he realised that West Ham United were never likely to be club that could fulfil that ambition. Derby's interest appeared to extend beyond Moore and they would also be interested in youngsters Frank Lampard and Trevor Brooking.

18th September 1973

A Board Meeting at West Ham United unanimously decided that, despite external pressure exerted by Derby's Manager, the press and Moore's own press comments, he would not be placed on the transfer list to the delight of his Manager, West Ham fans and players. This brought an end to five days of intense speculation.

21ˢᵗ *September 1973*

Against the increasing distrust between the Board and Manager, Derby followed up their initial interest in Henry Newton and signed him from Everton for a fee of £110,000, as usual, subject to passing a successful medical exam. The Club's doctor, Dr Cochrane, subsequently did the examination and told Clough that in his opinion Newton was likely to suffer from groin injuries and should not be signed. His recent playing record was not great, managing 74 appearances in three injury-hit seasons at Everton.

Clough failed to inform the Board, or Secretary of this medical advice and the player was signed regardless.

Newton, however, was pleased to be moving back to the Midlands, saying, 'I was very disappointed that Derby did not succeed in signing me in 1970. I reckon I've got three or four years left in the top grade.' He was to make his debut in Alan Durban's Testimonial match, against his former club Nottingham Forest, and his League debut in the away game at Tottenham Hotspur. Clough was pleased to add to his squad. 'I am sick of getting on the team coach and seeing the same 12 faces. It even got to the stage where players did not bother to look at the team sheet when it was pinned up.'

Luton Town had made an offer of £60,000 for defender Peter Daniel, which was turned down, and a day after the Newton signing and in the presence of Directors Kirkland and Rudd, the Manager was documented as saying, 'Southampton are anxious to buy Roger Davies and will give us £200,000 for him. We could get £400,000 for Davies and Gemmill; why the hell don't you give Peter and I a few quid and let us go and we will go quietly and not smear the club?'

Sir Alf Ramsey had named four Derby players in his squad for the coming match against Austria at Wembley on 26ᵗʰ September, which would then be followed by the must-win World Cup Qualification game against Poland in October. The four players were Roy McFarland, Colin Todd, David Nish and Kevin Hector, with Hector's inclusion in particular being met with universal press approval as a consistent scorer at the highest level.

During the last week of September, Michael Keeling had become concerned by the continuing approach adopted by the Chairman. He met with several Directors with a view that the Chairman should be asked if he thought it was time he resign, especially given his recent spell of ill health, and to see what could be done to repair the breakdown in communication and trust between Clough and himself.

Sir Robertson King, Mr Bradley and Mr Kirkland visited Sam Longson to see if he would step down, but no agreement was reached.

Monday 1ˢᵗ October 1973

It wasn't only the Derby Directors that were becoming concerned about the Manager, and Frank McGhee, writing his comment piece in the *Daily Mirror*, highlighted the dilemma that the Directors were faced with and brought it to the attention of football fans nationally. 'Maybe it is time busy, busy Brian Clough sorted out all his ambitions, all his priorities – and made up his mind about what he really wants to be. Right now he appears to be attempting three full-time roles – uninvited chief advisor to Sir Alf Ramsey; Soccer lecturer to the nation on ITV; and, with what time he has left, manager of Derby County.'

Brian Moore, the host of the ITV *On the Ball* show in which Clough appeared, also agreed with those sentiments. 'There is no doubt that Brian took his eye off the ball around that time – which was managing Derby – but we weren't complaining. Nor our viewers!'

Thursday 11ᵗʰ October 1973

Poland (England's remaining World Cup qualifying opponent) played a friendly in Amsterdam against the Netherlands, and Clough regarded it as an opportunity for some background research for being part of the ITV panel for the England game. Clough wanted to take Peter Taylor, and have the Club pay for all the expenses involved. Mr Longson agreed that they could go, provided the time away was deducted from their holiday entitlement and they paid for the trip themselves. Clough still submitted an expenses claim that was to remain unpaid.

The Board Meeting held was dominated by Mr Sam Longson's call for the Manager to be sacked with immediate effect. There was some opposition to this from other members of the Board, and he failed to get the majority he needed for that to be implemented.

Saturday 13ᵗʰ October 1973

With the close proximity of the crucial, deciding World Cup qualifier against Poland to be played on the following Wednesday, Clough made a valid comment to the press on the eve of the Manchester United away game, and one that is now commonplace: 'all matches involving England players this weekend should have been postponed. I said a month ago that it was ridiculous to play League games so close to the World Cup match.'

The Manchester United fixture at Old Trafford was to be their last, with Director Mr Jack Kirkland being the spark that was to lead to them resigning within a couple of days. He demanded to see Peter Taylor on the following Monday morning, in which he was to explain what job he actually does as the Assistant Manager, which upset the management pair, especially as this was coming from a relatively new Director who had not been involved with the club previously. There were several other incidents in and around the Directors' Box that afternoon that were cause for concern – a mix-up over tickets for Mrs Clough and Mrs Taylor, followed by a misunderstanding of a gesture made by the Manager in the direction of the Manchester United Chairman, Louis Edwards and Sir Matt Busby, that required the Manager to be brought up to the Directors' Box shortly afterwards to explain and apologise in person.

Since Mr Kirkland joined the Board some four months earlier (and was the largest shareholder of the football club), he had already formed an opinion, 'that the atmosphere within the club was poor, that there was an air of distrust between the Chairman and the Manager, and press attention was concentrated on the club, as a result of the Manager's activities.'

Sunday 14ᵗʰ October 1973

Once again it was suggested to Sam Longson by his fellow Directors that Clough and Taylor were no longer able to work with him and he should, for the good of the club, step aside as Chairman. Longson, in response, provided his own set of grievances against the Manager.

By this point both sides had become so entrenched with their respective positions it was impossible to see how the situation could be resolved, although Clough had been given ample time to simply provide the Board with details of his media commitments that would have satisfied the Chairman.

Monday 15ᵗʰ October 1973

The events of the day of their resignation, and the turmoil of the following days, have all been well documented many, many times from all of the major participants in their own books – Clough, Taylor, Longson, Stuart Webb, Don Shaw (Bring Back Clough campaign) and the man that typed their resignation letter, Derby *Evening Telegraph*'s Derby County reporter, Gerald Mortimer.

Director Michael Keeling, an ally of the management, resigned at the same time and lent his weight to the newly-formed protest movement that was to continue to fight for some time afterwards.

Clough and Taylor probably did not expect their resignations to be accepted and, realising their error, they tried to get themselves re-instated by approaching Director Sir Robertson King, asking him to take action to reverse the Board's decision and, if Sam Longson was to leave the Board of Directors, they would be willing to return to continue. Elsewhere, the town and local media were full of stories and rumours, and the shock and surprise sparked remarkable events amongst the players, who talked about going on strike and the fans were being organised to march through the streets in protest.

Thursday 18ᵗʰ October 1973

With Brian Clough attracting the attention and many pages in the national media, Chairman Sam Longson made a statement to the Derby *Evening Telegraph* in response:

The time has now come that the supporters of Derby County and in fact everyone concerned with football should hear my side. Just over two years ago, I was appointed Chairman for the second time and I found that we had a Secretary who was capable of carrying out the administration of the club. I therefore got the Board to agree that he should be put in complete charge of the administration. Mr Clough did not take too kindly to this move and criticised it in many ways. His first reaction was since I did not agree that he should take his family on the pre-season tour, he declined to go himself and failed therefore to fulfil his managerial duties. This was a very difficult situation.

He went on to make further comments about the Football Association complaints:

I begged the Manager to refrain before the club got into very serious trouble. He still persisted in this field and also ventured still further into television media. Events occurred that, to the Board, got near to a breach of Football League regulations and in the interests of Derby County I felt that any infringement of the FA and League rules would not, this time, be settled by a fine but could mean the club being expelled from the Football League and the Directors severely censured. When he stated that he was thinking of taking the ATV post just vacated by Jimmy Hill, I publicly stated that he would have to make up his mind whether he was carrying on as Manager of Derby County or taking this post. He stated later that he was not going to take the post, he was staying as Manager of Derby County. It came to our notice that he had taken a post with ATV, called it a different name, 'freelance commentator', and that he had taken a programme on a Saturday called *On the Ball*.

This necessitated him travelling down to London for these recordings and he was absent from two Board Meetings because of these appointments. The Board naturally was very concerned and asked him to give an account of these commitments and also reminded him of the clause in his contract which required him, amongst other things, to give his whole time and attention to the affairs of the club.

I received a letter from the Manager dated 24th September 1973, in which he stated that he had decided that to avoid any further confusion or misunderstanding regarding television, radio or newspaper work, he would not utter one single word to any of these media unless permission had first been obtained. Not for the first time by any means, he failed to keep his understanding. There followed letters, phone calls where he stated that both Peter Taylor and himself would go and not smear the Board if we would agree to some form of compensation and also give them their club cars. He also stated that he would sell one of the first team pool of players to provide the money for the compensation. We, of course, did not agree to this action as a Board.

We, therefore, informed him that unless he gave us in writing the particulars we required, the Board would take a very serious view of it. I say at this stage that we did not bar him from television, we merely asked that he must seek the Board's permission before taking any work and that he must honour his contract.

While the Manager states that this has all blown up in the last few weeks he is right in some respects that I would rather say it has been going on for two years and has come to a head in the last few weeks. Things have moved on rather quickly this last week or so, and he had embarked on a tyranny of abuse on myself and co-Directors, but I am afraid that on receiving his letter of resignation we had no alternative but to accept. I have had in the past many letters of resignation from him and many threats of leaving. He has said many times that Derby is not big enough for him. In the case of Coventry City, I was blackmailed into giving the Manager a £5,000 a year rise and the Assistant Manager £3,000. The Board and I have always met his demands and I myself very generously. The Manager's and Assistant Manager's salary for the last year came to over £40,000. This was without their television and press fees. He was allowed to carry on his activities from the club's offices, using all facilities, telephones, stationery and staff.

At the present point of time he is already due to appear before an FA Disciplinary Commission on serious charges due to press attacks on the FA and, even as late as last Saturday, at Old Trafford, he is alleged to have made what is now called 'the Harvey Smith gesture' to Mr Edwards, Chairman of United and to Sir Matt Busby, a Director. The Manager came up to the Boardroom and denied having done this. An official of the Football League told me at Wembley last night that Sir Matt Busby was under no illusion as to what took place.

Mr Clough has often insulted the supporters of Derby to the embarrassment of the Board and has often stated that he owes no loyalty to Derby, which is too small for him.

Nobody regrets the present situation more than I do. I brought him here, I have glorified in his success and I leave it with the supporters of Derby County to judge me and my Board. Hysteria is prevalent at present with some supporters. This is a position that he has created. It has been reported to me that he is receiving a considerable sum of money from the *Daily Mail* for a series of articles. Whether this is true or not, I cannot say. All in all, I say enough is enough.

Saturday 20ᵗʰ October 1973

The club's newspaper/programme, *The Ram*, for the first game following the resignations against Leicester City, carried a front and back page article and a full page inside stating the club's position, which is reproduced below:

Derby County had no alternative but to accept Brian Clough's resignation last Tuesday. Nor that of Peter Taylor, his Assistant Manager, who insisted on going with him.

For several months the Board of Directors had made a simple request of the Manager: tell us what press and television commitments you have. And we will tell you whether they conflict with your duties as Manager of Derby County FC. Every time Mr Clough was ambiguous in his reply, and never to the point, *even though his contract made crystal clear that all outside activities must be cleared by the Board.*

This week after several clashes, with this point as the main issue, he offered his resignation not for the first time. But it was the first time he offered it in writing, and this time it was accepted.

This must be stressed: the Board did not ask *Mr Clough to stop his outside work on newspapers and television.*

All that the Board repeatedly asked him was this: tell us your obligations so that we may know whether they conflict with the Derby County commitments recorded in your contract.

There was also a larger issue involved. Just over a year ago the Football League Management Committee called the Chairman Mr Sam Longson in front of them to tell them they were disturbed by many of the statements coming from Mr Clough.

To safeguard the image of football, the clubs have framed a rule prohibiting people employed inside the game from attacking their colleagues. It is widely accepted by managers, players and officials.

Mr Longson was reminded by the League that Derby County alone were responsible for the actions of all the people employed by them.

Even though the club asked to know of Mr Clough's intentions with the media mainly to satisfy themselves that the best interests of both the shareholders and the supporters were being maintained, they were also aware of the risks they were running with the Establishment. It was known that the Football Association were also concerned about the Manager's criticisms.

The situation had to be regularised for the sake of the club, if not that of the Manager. As a matter of principle, they expected to know what his press and TV commitments were. At no time would Mr Clough comply with their request.

Many times before there have been behind-the-scenes difficulties for the Board to resolve. Several times before Mr. Clough has tendered his resignation. *On every occasion the Board has, after a great deal of consideration, reached a compromise. This time it was not possible.*

The reaction of Chairman, Mr Sam Longson, the man who brought the pair here in the first place was: 'It is a sad day, and we all bitterly regret their going. We can only thank Brian Clough and Peter Taylor for he great job of work they did for us.'

When the early shock impact has died down the departures will be clearly seen as a stepping stone in the club's history and the end of an era.

THE CLUB IS CERTAIN THAT THE BULK OF OUR PUBLIC WILL CONTINUE THEIR TREMENDOUS SUPPORT TO THE PLAYERS WHO ARE, AFTER ALL, THE REAL BACKBONE OF ANY SUCCESSFUL CLUB.

The full-page article on the inside pages expands further on the lead story in the paper:

The parting of the ways between Derby County, Brian Clough and Peter Taylor this week was something which the Board of the club regret as much, perhaps even more, than any of their supporters. *But it was something which could not be avoided, in the Board's view.*

And one thing needs to be stressed: the Board have never refused to allow Mr Clough to write for the newspapers, or to appear on television. Everybody connected with the club was delighted they were getting so much exposure, so much publicity through the Manager. But what the

Board did do was to repeatedly request Mr Clough to give them details of his press and TV commitments in accordance with his contract with the club. *Had he complied, the Directors could have judged whether or not they were likely to interfere with his clearly-defined duties and commitments to Derby County FC.*

They could also have advised Mr Clough whether he was likely to be putting himself at risk with football's authorities. This request he found himself unable to agree with. It is inevitably ignored by the critics, but of great concern to everybody in the game, that people employed in the industry do not attack either their colleagues in football, or the administration.

This is a Football League ruling which was framed by the clubs themselves in the interests of the public image of League football. It protects everyone employed, either full time or part time, within Association Football, and no-one is excepted from its obligations.

As we state on our front page the Football League, as long ago as last year, asked Mr Longson to appear before them to discuss the outside activities of Mr Clough. He was, they said, indulging in criticisms of the League and its clubs which could not be accepted. *Derby County were reminded of their responsibilities to football.*

This was several months ago. Since then Mr Clough widened his horizons to include criticisms of both the Football Association and Sir Alf Ramsey. More, he expanded his field beyond the national Press by taking on an appointment with ITV as their freelance spokesman.

While the Board were delighted that their Manager's efforts to widen the publicity for club affairs had been as successful as his work with the team itself, they became increasingly worried about the effect on the club of these constant clashes with Authority. They considered that if Mr Clough allowed them to be informed of his various activities, as his contract stipulated, they could advise him on matters which a Club Manager should preferably not involve himself with.

The Derby County image, and consequently that of Mr Clough himself, was their only concern. Mr Clough did not interpret their efforts that way.

And most certainly does not now. He could not agree that the Board was only imposing its right, according to contract, of ensuring that the welfare of Derby County on and off the field was the primary consideration.

Yet this was, and remains to the end, the only serious disagreement between the Manager and the club.

Following repeated pressure from the Board for Mr Clough to accede to their requests he finally tendered his resignation this week ... a decision which the Board felt they had no alternative but to accept, considering all the circumstances.

The Board stress that they accepted the resignation of both Mr Clough and Mr Taylor with sincere regret, particularly as the Board had striven unceasingly to resolve the situation. And they pay tribute to the great work which both men have done for the club since they came to the Baseball Ground six years ago.

The man who is the most unhappy of them all is the Chairman, Mr Sam Longson, who was instrumental in bringing the partnership to Derby County.

'This is a sad day for me,' he said to *The Ram*, 'but in the end we were left with no alternative. All we wanted was for Mr Clough to manage our club as brilliantly as he has always done, but this was no longer enough.'

The Chairman has spent six years praising Mr Clough and Mr Taylor for the job they have done at the Baseball Ground. *No-one has defended their cause as he has done . . . no-one has fought harder to keep them with Derby County.*

But this week, at last, he had to give the situation best. 'No-one can be bigger than the club,' he said. 'No-one can put the club's interests second.'

THE PARTING OF THE WAYS, IN THE END WAS INEVITABLE.

Monday 22nd October 1973

Following the statement released by the Board, Clough immediately starting legal proceedings against all of the football club's Directors who were in office on 18th October in the High Court (Case No. 7356) for damages for alleged libel. There followed several months of evidence-gathering, statement-giving and lots of solicitors' time, and money from both sides.

Despite the evidence weighing heavily against Clough, it was thought by the majority of the Directors that it was in everyone's best interests to settle the matter out of court, to keep legal fees to a minimum and to minimise any potential harm to their own business interests and personal reputations as well as that of the Club. Chairman Longson was against this settlement, believing it would look like they were admitting defeat and taking some degree of fault, but eventually, some two years after the resignations had taken place, the club paid Clough an out-of-court settlement figure of around £10,000.

Wednesday 24th October 1973

The headline in the Derby *Evening Telegraph* read: 'The Clough saga is over' as Dave Mackay is appointed as the new Manager.

Saturday 27th October 1973

For only the second time since *The Ram* newspaper/programme was launched, it was issued prior to an away game (West Ham United) on 27th October. The front page summed up the feelings from within the club:

You will find no boasts or promises from Mr Mackay in *The Ram*. You know he is not that sort of man. There are no threats against, or promises to, the players as a result of their off-field activities this week. Everyone appreciates loyalty, and that has been demonstrated.

Our only hope, the hope of everyone, is that we can now get back to the football.

You will find no recriminations against anyone in this issue of *The Ram*. Much has been said elsewhere. Let it remain there.

Our job is to look forward, not back. Our job is to welcome Mr Mackay to the Baseball Ground as Manager, and to pass this message to our supporters: football goes on, it must go on.

How, where and why now depends on Mr Mackay and his players.

	HOME			**AWAY**	

League Diision 1

25/08/1973	Chelsea	1–0	01/09/1973	Birmingham City	0–0
29/08/1973	Manchester City	1–0	04/09/1973	Liverpool	0–2
08/09/1973	Everton	2–1	15/09/1973	Burnley	1–1
12/09/1973	Liverpool	3–1	18/09/1973	Coventry City	0–1
22/09/1973	Southampton	6–2	29/09/1973	Tottenham Hotspur	0–1
06/10/1973	Norwich City	1–1	13/10/1973	Manchester United	1–0
20/10/1973	Leicester City	2–1	27/10/1973	West Ham United	0–0
03/11/1973	QPR	1–2	10/11/1973	Ipswich Town	0–3
24/11/1973	Leeds United	0–0	17/11/1973	Sheffield United	0–3
08/12/1973	Arsenal	1–1	15/12/1973	Newcastle United	2–0
22/12/1973	Tottenham Hotspur	2–0	26/12/1973	Stoke City	0–0
01/01/1974	Birmingham City	1–1	29/12/1973	Everton	1–2
12/01/1974	Burnley	5–1	19/01/1974	Chelsea	1–1
02/02/1974	Newcastle United	1–0	06/02/1974	Manchester City	0–1
16/02/1974	Manchester United	2–2	23/02/1974	Norwich City	4–2
02/03/1974	Stoke City	1–1	05/03/1974	Southampton	1–1
09/03/1974	West Ham United	1–1	16/03/1974	Leicester City	1–0
23/03/1974	Ipswich Town	2–0	30/03/1974	QPR	0–0
13/04/1974	Sheffield United	4–1	06/04/1974	Leeds United	0–2
15/04/1974	Coventry City	1–0	09/04/1974	Wolverhampton Wanderers	0–4
27/04/1974	Wolverhampton Wanderers	2–0	20/04/1974	Arsenal	0–2

League Cup

| 08/10/1973 | Sunderland | 2–2 | 29/10/1973 | Sunderland | 1–1 |
| | | | 31/10/1973 | Sunderland | 0–3 |

FA Cup

| 05/01/1974 | Boston United | 0–0 | 09/01/1974 | Boston United | 6–1 |
| 30/01/1974 | Coventry City | 0–1 | 27/01/1974 | Coventry City | 0–0 |

Friendlies

| | | | 08/08/1973 | Merthyr Tydfill | 3–1 |

	15/08/1973	VFL Osnabruck	1–0
	18/08/1973	Benfica	1–2
	19/08/1973	Atletico Madrid	2–1
	22/04/1974	Kettering	2–1
	May 1974	Coventry/ Everton	1–1/ 2–2

Testimonials

26/09/1974	Nottm Forest (Durban)	1–1		03/12/1973	Bristol City (Sharpe)	1–0
25/02/1974	Spartak Moscow (Hennessey)	1–3		06/05/1974	Leicester City (Cross)	2–2

SEASON SUMMARY

Football League Division One:	3rd
FA Cup:	Fourth Round
Football League Cup:	Second Round
National 5-a-Side:	Semi-final
Average League Attendance:	27,788
Highest Attendance:	36,003 v. Leeds United
Top League Scorers:	Hector (19)
	Davies (9)
	Bourne (7)

ND - #0265 - 270225 - C0 - 234/156/15 - PB - 9781780915487 - Gloss Lamination